W9-BFF-900

the
Big
Move

the Big Move

Life Between the
Turning Points

〜〜〜〜

Anne M. Wyatt-Brown,
Ruth Ray Karpen, and
Helen Q. Kivnick

WITH AN AFTERWORD BY
Margaret Morganroth Gullette

INDIANA UNIVERSITY PRESS
Bloomington & Indianapolis

This book is a publication of

Indiana University Press
Office of Scholarly Publishing
Herman B Wells Library 350
1320 East 10th Street
Bloomington, Indiana 47405 USA

iupress.indiana.edu

*Manufactured in the
United States of America*

*Library of Congress
Cataloging-in-Publication Data*

Names: Wyatt-Brown, Anne M., 1939–
  author. | Ray, Ruth E., 1954– author.
  | Kivnick, Helen Q., author.
Title: The big move : life between the
  turning points / by Anne M. Wyatt-
  Brown, Ruth Ray Karpen, and Helen
  Q. Kivnick ; with an afterword by
  Margaret Morganroth Gullette.
Description: Bloomington : Indiana
  University Press, [2016] | Includes
  bibliographical references and index.
Identifiers: LCCN 2015036115| ISBN
  9780253020642 (pbk. : alk. paper)
  | ISBN 9780253020734 (ebook)
Subjects: LCSH: Wyatt-Brown, Anne
  M., 1939– | Life care communities—
  Maryland. | Retirement
  communities—Maryland. | Older
  people—Maryland—Social
  conditions. | Older people—Care—
  Maryland. | Caregivers—Maryland.
  | Life change events—Maryland.
Classification: LCC HV1454.2.U62
  M359 2016 | DDC 362.61092—dc23
LC record available at http://
lccn.loc.gov/2015036115

1 2 3 4 5   21 20 19 18 17 16

Contents

INTRODUCTION

Home Places

Ruth Ray Karpen

More and more Americans are retiring to new places. Surveys by the American Association of Retired People find that as many as 60–80 percent of baby boomers plan to move in retirement. They are looking for more temperate climates, affordable lifestyles, good health care, and opportunities for part-time work and volunteering. These changes often involve simplifying, downsizing and moving closer to children and grandchildren. They represent a turning point from the midlife engagements of work, career building, and child rearing to later life engagements yet to be determined.

The "big move" in our title refers to an even more dramatic change: the move to a continuing-care retirement community (CCRC), where residents can get more assistance as their health declines. These communities offer a continuum of care, from little or none for residents living independently in homes or apartments, to full custodial and nursing care for those living in the health center or nursing facility. Despite the wide range of care needs, the fascinating diversity of residents, and the range of amenities most places offer, the CCRC still carries some of the stigma of the dreaded "old age home" of yesteryear, where couples could be separated and care was negligent.

Age researchers who study "environmental gerontology" are particularly interested in how older people interact within these new environments to create and maintain a sense of identity, agency, and belonging (Wahl et al. 2012). They wonder how new residents manage to turn an undifferentiated space, such as an apartment or room, into a specific and personal place that feels like "home." Gerontologists find that, throughout our lives, but especially in later life, our ability to create these home places is affected by many factors outside our own control: "Processes of making and remaking place by both individual and social groups are facilitated or hampered by environmental design, by models of social care and human service practices and, on a larger scale, by public policy" (Rowles and Bernard 2013, xii). A single story of relocation like the one at the center of this book beautifully illustrates how crucial it is for all of us to grow old in social environments where we can flourish even as we or those we love need more care.

Being able to create and maintain a home in later life is an important social and environmental issue because the American population is aging, and older adults spend as much as 80 percent of their time at home. As we become frailer, we occupy increasingly less space within that home—a process gerontologists call "environmental centralization." Where we once occupied an entire house, many of us will eventually live in one or two rooms, then an area within one room, and finally perhaps a single chair or bed (Rowles and Bernard

2013, 13). The more comfortable and "at home" we feel in these increasingly smaller places, the more likely we will be to live out our days with a sense of well-being. And, paradoxically, the feeling that we are "in place" and at home may help us better release the world when death draws near (Rowles and Bernard 2013, 17).

Big moves that represent turning points in our lives, such as going off to college, joining the military, getting married, buying a first home, or moving into a CCRC, pose many challenges to our sense of identity and belonging. Some of us are more adept at creating new homes than others are. Gerontologists have found that "abandonment of a familiar home and remaking a sense of being in place and at home in a new setting is not only stressful, but also a skill" (Rowles and Bernard 2013, 14). Moving into new places requires not only researching, organizing, planning, and prioritizing, but also navigating new spaces, engaging in new activities, making friends, choosing whether to pursue new opportunities and occupations, and developing new habits and routines. One must be willing and able to balance the constraints and opportunities of the new environment to create a new way of being "in place and at home," while also letting go of some of the previous ways of being at the place and home one left behind (Rowles and Bernard 2013, 14). The stressors are magnified for those who have less physiological or psychological reserve than others, or less experience changing environments, and are less able to adapt. Others do better than they or anyone expected.

The Big Move pivots around the story of one woman's move to a CCRC. Anne Wyatt-Brown, a retired linguistics professor and gerontologist, tells the story of her move to a community in Baltimore called Roland Park Place. At seventy-one, she was healthy and able—and one of the youngest residents in the community—while her husband Bert, seventy-eight, had a serious lung disease and needed care. Anne describes how she navigates this new environment, first with apprehension and some resistance, distancing herself from the residents in wheelchairs, and gradually making friends and getting involved in the community.

Anne and Bert did have advantages that made their adjustment easier. They were a financially comfortable middle-class couple with intellectual resources. They had done their homework and carefully selected this community based on location, reputation, and previous family members' experiences. Roland Park Place also had amenities that appealed to them in particular: a café where residents could congregate outside the more formal dining room, a fitness center (Anne and Bert had worked out together throughout their marriage), and opportunities to participate in shaping the environment and governing the community. Many of the residents were retired professionals with whom they shared intellectual and cultural interests. Several of their family members lived nearby, and Anne could roam the city on her own and at will. Among the youngest and most able residents, Anne and Bert could still travel to national conferences and continue their academic work. In other words, their world would not be just the continuing-care community, as it was for some of the other residents.

Still, Anne and Bert went through profound physical and emotional changes, and in Chapter 1, Anne is forthright and strikingly honest in describing them. She offers insight and practical advice to readers wanting a first-hand account of how to adjust to life in a retirement community.

Following Anne's chapter, three of her colleagues analyze her story and explain its larger significance. The commentators demonstrate how personal stories, read carefully through the lens of research and theory, can deepen, enliven and enrich our understanding of life in general, and later life in particular.

This book began in 2011, when Anne presented a talk to fellow scholars attending the 64th annual meeting of the Gerontological Society of America. She recounted her recent move to a CCRC. Her talk was followed by commentary from three scholars, all members of the Humanities and Arts subcommittee of the Gerontological Society of America: Helen Kivnick, a developmental and clinical psychologist from the University of Minnesota; Kate DeMedeiros, a narrative gerontologist from Miami University; and Ruth Ray (now Ruth Ray Karpen), an English professor and feminist gerontologist from Wayne State University. The session was a uniquely personal contribution to that rarefied, academic environment, and the audience responded enthusiastically. Margaret Morganroth Gullette, an independent scholar, cultural critic, and friend of Anne's, was in the audience and responded warmly, suggesting then and there that the group should write a book. Anne agreed to expand on and publish her story, and three of us—Helen, Ruth, and Margaret—were inspired to continue our commentary. Taken together, Anne's story and our responses—all informed by personal interests and experience as well as professional knowledge—are a creative alternative to the more conventional research-based forms of writing and knowledge making in gerontology. We are all humanistic gerontologists and, as such, look for ways to make aging and old age more understandable and relatable on a human level. We care about the thoughts and feelings of older people themselves, and we try to describe old age from inside the experience. We are also committed to improving the ways that American society views aging and cares for old people.

Readers will find many lessons, both simple and profound, in this slim volume. One in particular stands out as a central truth: even as we grow old, we do not stop growing. Though difficult and often painful, a big move can challenge us to grow in unexpected ways. Anne Wyatt-Brown discovered this herself, and it was a happy surprise. In moving to Roland Park Place, she thought she was making a loving sacrifice for her husband of fifty years. But it turned out to be one of the best things to happen in her life, too.

REFERENCES

Rowles, Graham D., and Miriam Bernard, eds. 2013. Environmental Gerontology: Making Meaningful Places in Old Age. New York: Springer.

Wahl, Hans-Werner, Suzanne Iwarsson, and Frank Oswald. 2012. "Aging Well and the Environment: Toward an Integrative Model and Research Agenda for the Future." Gerontologist 52: 306–16.

ONE

A Wife's Life,
A Humanist's Journey,
2010–2012
Anne M. Wyatt-Brown

What is it like for a relatively young and healthy person to move into a continuing-care retirement community when most of the other residents are much older and many are sick? This is the life change that I report on here. It strikes me as a task worth attempting because few accounts exist from those who currently live in a similar place. Most of the accounts that have been published are about the not-so-recent past or were written by visitors rather than permanent residents. Joyce Horner, for example, wrote a wrenching account (*That Time of Year* [1982]) of three years in a nursing home in the 1970s. She moved in because of crippling arthritis, and she appeared to be one of the few residents whose mind was still alert. Two more recent books give an accurate picture of what communities of elders were like in the late 1990s and early twenty-first century, but neither writer actually resided permanently in the institution.

The first by Ruth Ray, *Endnotes* (2008), describes her relationship with an eighty-two-year-old male resident of a nursing home called Bedford. To her surprise, she fell in love with him. She spent so much time at Bedford that she learned what life was like for other residents as well. The second by Dudley Clendinen, *A Place Called Canterbury* (2008), describes life in a retirement home in Florida where his mother, who had suffered a massive stroke, resided during her final years. These books are well worth reading, but the places they describe differ considerably from our facility. For example, Susan Reimer's review of Clendinen's book mentions that wheelchairs were not permitted in the Canterbury dining room. Moreover, his mother's friends deserted her when she had to move from independent living to the health care facility (Reimer 2008). The community where my husband Bert and I moved, Roland Park Place, allows wheelchairs in the dining room, and most people in the health care center continue to visit their friends.

Roland Park Place is one of the few continuing care places in the city of Baltimore. Most of the other retirement communities are in the outlying countryside. It is older than many of the other facilities, but it is well maintained and has a wonderfully caring staff. Our campus consists of one large building of eight stories. There are three levels of care: independent living, assisted living, and health care for those who need skilled nursing. Most of the more than three hundred residents live in their own apartments, some with nursing assistance from women called Pals, paid for by the resident. Because this is a continuing-care community, residents may stay here, regardless of worsening health, until they die.

Unlike people in retirement communities that have sprung up on Florida golf courses, at least half of the residents in Roland Park Place are not only old, but also suffer from varying degrees of frailty. One might ask why frailty is widespread in this community. The situation is influenced by several factors. Americans value their independence at every stage of life, even as they grow older. Some in their eighties and nineties resist the idea of moving into a senior apartment of any kind until a drastic illness makes such change necessary. The media encourages this resistance by paying attention to the behavior of baby boomers, many of whom are too young to think they need any kind of assistance. As a result, they attempt some other joint living arrangement (Carrns 2011; Pope 2011). What many don't realize is that a facility like ours will allow people to remain independent as long as possible and then stay in the same place when they need skilled nursing care. If "aging in place" is desirable, then moving at a younger age may be less traumatic than moving later at a time of crisis. Ironically, while writing a draft of this chapter, I received an e-mail from the American Society on Aging announcing a web seminar describing technology to enable seniors to age in place.

Of course, it is cheaper and easier for people to stay in their houses rather than enter nursing homes. With technological advances, stay-at-home elders may be much safer than they have been in the past. Unfortunately, the problem of isolation remains, especially for those who can no longer drive. After all, technology does not provide live companionship and intellectual stimulation. Alas, few nursing homes attempt to meet these needs. For a compatible social group, one needs to move into a continuing-care facility while one is still relatively healthy; to do so, one must find a place that is affordable.

Although my husband and I had already given the matter of where to dwell in old age a good deal of thought, our decision to move was precipitated by events beyond our control. In 2004, we had retired from the University of Florida and moved to Baltimore. I had grown up in the city, and both Bert and I had attended graduate school at Johns Hopkins. We bought a condo on Stony Run Lane from my sister. It consisted of half a house, which had been built in 1904 and renovated in the 1970s. It was a lovely old building with three sets of stairs, causing us to run from the basement to the third floor. Unfortunately, Bert was diagnosed with pulmonary fibrosis in December 2006. It is a progressive lung disease, and over time, he found climbing the stairs harder and harder.

In the winter of 2010, we had two enormous snowstorms, referred to locally as "snowmaggedon." Five years later, the *Baltimore Sun* still displays pictures of the storm with stories that the reporters describe as "life-changing events." I can testify that the storms certainly changed our lives. Before the snow had become too deep, we had flown to Florida to visit friends. Upon returning, we were unable to drive onto Stony Run Lane, a one-way street that goes down a steep hill. The city rarely bothers to plow it because only two houses and some apartment complexes are on it. Our house was the only one that lacked any alternative place to park. We ended up renting a parking place from one of the apartment buildings, but Bert had to climb two flights to get up to street level and walk across to where we lived. At that point, he announced that he would not spend another winter in the house.

We had long since made up our minds that when the time came we would move into Roland Park Place. My parents had lived there in the 1980s and 1990s. Of course, we thought we would have many years before that day arrived. Our half of the house on Stony Run Lane needed work before it could be sold, and we had to hope that Roland Park Place could accommodate us.

As it happened we were lucky. Roland Park Place was able to give us a suitable apartment, and we were even luckier to sell our condo in July 2010, despite a terrible market.

Roland Park Place is a five-minute drive from our old place. This made it easy for me to go back and forth between the two many times. I was unprepared, however, for what the move would entail emotionally. We were both in our seventies— I was seventy-one and Bert was seventy-eight—and when I learned that the average age of residents was eighty-five, I told the interviewer rather facetiously that I might "study" the inhabitants as a gerontologist. This remark suggests that living among the "old-old," as I then thought of them, was not an enticing proposition.

I remembered that my mother had never adjusted to her new life in Roland Park Place. In contrast, my father had loved being there. He went down to dinner every night and met many new people. Unfortunately, he died a few months after arriving. We found unpacked boxes under my mother's bed when she died in 1993, six years after moving in. Of course, widowhood was hard for her, as she had lost her one contact with the wider community. What contributed most to her unhappiness was her bad eyesight. She was nearly blind and kept to her apartment to avoid being rude to someone she could not see.

The place was quite different in the late 1980s and early 1990s from what it is today. The residents dressed more formally than we do, and elaborate cocktail parties were the norm in some circles. When my parents had lived there, most residents were reasonably fit, at least initially. In those days, most people had to walk in to be admitted to the independent living section. Of course, exceptions were made if one person in a family needed to move into residential care. In contrast, fewer people who move in now are in good shape physically. When a new couple arrives, usually one of them needs more help than the other. In our case, upon arrival, Bert dragged an oxygen concentrator and found walking any distance tiring. As a friend who is wheelchair-bound remarked with only some exaggeration, we are less a "retirement community" than a "disability community." Fortunately, since my mother's time, Roland Park Place has added ambulatory care and a fitness center with a swimming pool. They have also extended the health care section considerably.

When Bert and I first moved into Roland Park Place on May 20, 2010, I discovered that being a humanistically inclined gerontologist did not help me overcome my initially negative feelings about our new dwelling. On one of our first nights in the dining room, when I saw the lineup of walkers stretching around the corner, I thought, "What on earth am I doing in a place like this?" That evening, however, behind my back, I heard a very interesting conversation between two women. When I saw one of them leave the dining room, I discovered that she was using a walker. I also noticed that walkers reduced the potential number of wheelchairs that otherwise would have dotted the landscape.

Gradually I began to find ways of getting to know other residents. I developed strategies for meeting people. When lacking dinner partners, we would see if we could team up with people outside the dining room so that we wouldn't eat alone. That often worked well. I started a list of people I had met to help me remember their names. Before long I had met about eighty people and had begun to remember their names and stories. We went to some weekend coffee hours and met those who attend regularly. Swimming aerobic classes were small, about six to ten people, so I become good friends with my classmates. Moreover, swimming and coffee hours are good places to collect useful gossip. A month after the move, I looked around the dining room and realized I knew several people and felt more at home.

We are lucky that our facility includes many retired doctors, professors, and other professionals, but some of the most amusing people are interested in athletics, drama, or other pursuits. In November 2010, I competed for a turkey by exercising as many hours as possible. I was defeated by Maggie Weinberg, a ninety-five-year-old woman who devoted all of her time to the competition. In 2011, the fitness people asked us to exercise for as many miles as possible, and once again Maggie outstripped my efforts. She told me that her fitness had improved dramatically because of our friendly competition. Sadly, Maggie died in January 2012. After her remembrance service, Maggie's daughter told me how much pleasure it had given her mother to defeat me, a much younger woman.

Thanks to another resident named Lawson, who had been active with her husband in Baltimore's drama world, we planned a dramatic reading of *Spoon River* for November 2010. Unfortunately, the man who was to lend us a sound system had to postpone the loan, and the date was changed to January. Just before Christmas Lawson's husband, Bob, the lead performer, died. Lawson rescheduled the reading for January 29, and her son substituted for her husband. The performance went beautifully, but we were all reminded of how tentative our plans—and our lives—really are.

Fairly soon I discovered that the café was a great place to have lunch on a regular basis, and I found myself impressed by how the other residents treated each other. I noticed the kindness of many who cheerfully ate with those who were in wheelchairs or had spotty memories. We began eating regularly with two people in wheelchairs, as well as an old friend whose stroke inhibits her speech and makes it impossible for her to walk. Of course, maneuvering walkers and wheelchairs through the café at lunchtime resembles dodge ball, but that is the small price we pay for rich sociability. Six or eight of us sometimes crowd around a table built for four and exchange gossip, complaints, and stories from our lives and those of others. At times we talk politics because most of us are Democrats and reasonably liberal. When a resident has a genuine gripe, it helps to be able to share the story and receive support. People confide in each other if they feel that others are genuinely interested in their situation. Sometimes, one discovers that the person to whom one is talking doesn't remember salient details of the conversation, yet the telling can still be cathartic. Many people eat dinner regularly with a special friend whom they keep an eye on.

It didn't take too long before I stopped merely observing the community and began feeling like part of the group. Taking part in other organized activities, such as swimming classes, hikes, and bus trips, introduced me to many other residents. In time, I was asked to serve on the editorial board of *The Residents' Review*, which produces some remarkably good essays. I also joined the Fitness Committee, where we make suggestions for improvements that might be implemented in the future. Joining a vigil group for peace on Fridays gave me yet another group with whom to talk. People from the neighboring community join our weekly vigil and lunch with us in the café afterward. I have been delighted by their conversation, which covers a broad range of topics including politics.

During the summer of 2011, I joined a caregivers' monthly meeting, which introduced me to many people who are caring for demented spouses. At first I worried that I wouldn't fit well into this group because Bert was of sound mind. As it has happened, though, I received very useful advice from the other participants, especially about airplane travel when one person is on oxygen. I think they enjoy hearing about problems for which they can offer positive solutions. At the same time, I have been impressed by the coping skills of the other caregivers, their sense of humor, and their affection for their husbands or wives. Katie Miller, the social worker who facilitates the group, seeks to mitigate our problems by offering useful, practical advice.

Based on our experience choosing a continuing-care facility, I have some suggestions for picking a suitable place for oneself or one's family members. Try not to leave the decision until a crisis occurs. If you as a parent want to be near your children, think of moving to the new town while you are still active. Some of the people we have met moved here directly from another state, but doing so complicates the relocation process. For example, one of our wheelchair-bound friends can no longer drive. She has no idea where anything outside of our building might be. This adds disorientation to her adjustment.

Another strategy is to visit people that you know who have already gone into a local retirement community. We were lucky on that front. We knew only one other couple when we moved in, but I had grown up in Baltimore and had many elderly relatives. Over the years, I saw improvements in the choices that older people had. One of my aunts had moved happily from her apartment to a Quaker-run establishment in Hunt Valley, Maryland. Another lived for many years in a place similar to ours in Towson, Maryland. Both were pleased with their choices. We visited them several times and had a chance to evaluate the relative strengths and weaknesses of each place. We realized, however, that we are city people who want to live near our old neighborhood in Baltimore. Luckily for us, Roland Park Place is close to my brother, sister-in-law, and my sister, as well as to some of their children.

Even more important, if possible, find out how the staff treats the residents. Most of the members of our staff are extremely helpful and courteous. We assume that the staff is treated well by the management, which would explain why they are so kind to the residents. Also ask how the cost of the place will increase if a person needs skilled nursing. Some places charge less to those in independent living and a good deal more to residents in the equivalent of a nursing home. And avoid for-profit institutions if possible. Certain medical tax deductions are available only to those who live in a not-for-profit facility.

In time, I came to see that age is far from being the only salient factor in adjusting to life in a continuing-care community. Some residents in their eighties and nineties do have a hard time adjusting. Others who are much younger may adjust more quickly, especially if they need the support of the institution. My husband, like many others whose health is impaired, was relieved to make the move. To try and figure out what factors are significant, I've been considering my feelings and observing the behavior and conversations of those around me. I've also consulted residents who moved in about the time that we did. Those who relocated to get care for an ailing spouse sometimes harbor regrets about the decision. A few months ago, a resident told us at coffee hour that he wished he could still live in the apartment building where he and his wife had lived before the move. His wife is virtually blind and in ill health, so he had no choice. He takes part in many activities, however, and is well liked by the other residents.

I talked briefly to Katie Miller, the social worker, about this question of adjustment. She agreed that age is not the only variable. People bring themselves to a new place with all their own strengths and weaknesses. Some have learned to adjust to changing circumstances; others feel overwhelmed. My guess is that if one reaches out to others, it takes less time to feel at home. I really can't predict how long adjustment takes because it's different for everyone.

In my case, after living at Roland Park Place for two years, I can see that my feelings will probably continue to change depending on what is going on in my life and the lives of those around me, especially Bert's. I am grateful that we can obtain intelligent medical advice without leaving the building. The many elevators make Bert's life much easier. My ambivalence is not surprising in view of the mixture of positive and negative factors involved in living in a continuing-care community. On the plus side, we've made a lot of friends, several in their nineties, who have told me marvelous stories about their youth. Nearly a year ago, a resident suggested that life here is like a dry cruise. At times it can almost feel like being in college, especially when we talk to friends in the laundry room. On the other hand, a recent widow reported how difficult it is for her when she goes into her apartment and shuts the door. One can feel very alone, even in a large community, unless there is a lively person sharing one's space.

On the minus side, living here reminds me that the rest of the world tends to dismiss those of us who no longer live in ordinary housing. One woman told a resident that she had eaten meals with her mother when she was in a place like ours, and that she had no intention of repeating the experience. The food at Roland Park Place is fine, but the woman clearly does not like being around frail elders with their walkers and wheelchairs. Some residents have felt humiliated when a friend on the outside said, "Oh, do you still drive?" as if all normal activities ended when they moved into the retirement community. Probably those people are scared of what the future might hold for them. They fear being forced to confront images of their future.

As one's health declines, being made to move into assisted living can cause an upset. One woman I barely knew complained loudly that her children forced her to give up her apartment. She obviously felt that she had lost control of her life. Of course, we see painful signs of the future, consisting of disability, decline, and death. Fortunately, we have friends to share these observations with, and staff members, especially those in ambulatory care or the rehabilitation center, who work hard to help us overcome disability and decline. The staff attempts to postpone death as long as possible.

Our situation has changed since we moved in. A few months ago we decided that Bert needed a motorized wheelchair because his breathing is more labored. We discovered that it takes two to three months to get one, but fortunately the company has given him a loaner. Now he can go anywhere in the building or outside if it is not raining. Shortly after he started using his loaner, a friend came hurrying over to our table in the dining room in his wheelchair to compare notes about the two machines. Both Bert and I found that act of solidarity to be very comforting. When staff members Valencio Jackson and Stuart Edwards, who run the fitness and aquatics centers, saw that Bert was using a chair, they told me what exercises he needs to do to keep his legs strong.

Our Roland Park Place friends who are adjusting to worsening health sometimes inspire us. My friend Betty, who was in independent living and the leader of the Friday peace vigil, was unexpectedly stricken with severe back pain. She has temporarily moved into the health care center and has been using a wheelchair for five or six weeks. Unfortunately, her legs no longer work as efficiently as they once did. If things do not improve, she will have to move into assisted living or stay in health care. She told me recently that as long as she can continue to write her memoir, she will be all right. I was impressed by her equanimity. Because the health care center is in the same building as independent living, many of Betty's friends from the building and the Friday vigil continue to visit. That helps keep up her spirits.

As a result of interaction with other residents, I have learned to put a human face on problems that I had only read about in novels, memoirs, and gerontology books. Last fall at the café, I had some heart-to-heart conversations with Alice Steinbach, a retired journalist who was slowly dying from metastasized cancer. For many years, Alice had been well known in Baltimore. She was the first female journalist at the Baltimore *Sun* to be awarded a Pulitzer Prize. I had not lived in Baltimore from 1962 until 2004, so at first I had no idea of her fame. What impressed me was her willingness to discuss her horrible prognosis. Many people at Roland Park Place do not want the subject of death even to be raised obliquely. Alice talked to me openly of her situation and expressed concern for my husband's declining health.

Toward the end of her life, I joined two friends, Lawson and Michael, in reading to Alice, who needed distraction from her slow path to death. Lawson had known Alice some years ago, and Michael had started to converse with her when they both moved in across the hall from each other. We could not make the pain go away, but we found a way to give her meaningful pleasure. Early on, Alice declared that she wanted to die immediately, but after watching my mother's final illness in 1993, I knew that death was not imminent. Realizing that Alice was eager to talk about her existential situation, I read poems that we had discussed in poetry class at Roland Park Place, some of which dealt with death and dying.

Michael and Lawson are wonderful readers and picked inspired choices. Michael lent Alice a biography of Rachel Carson that described how she reacted to the one-year-life cycle of monarch butterflies, when she was dying of breast cancer (Lear 1997). Carson delighted to think that she, like the monarchs, was part of the natural world. She wrote Dorothy Freeman, her closest friend, in 1963: "For the Monarch, that cycle is measured in a known span of months. For ourselves, the measure is something else, the span of which we cannot know. But the thought is the same: when that intangible cycle has run its course it is a natural and not unhappy thing that a life comes to an end" (http://www.lettersofnote.com/2014/04/dear-one. htmlwww.boothbayharborblog.com). Alice returned to that passage repeatedly, sometimes reading it to us and other times listening to us read it.

Several times, Lawson read parts of E. B. White's *Charlotte's Web*, which we all enjoyed. In the morning hours before Alice died, Lawson read the final chapter of A. A. Milne's *The House at Pooh Corner* ([1928] 1961). Attracted by the reading, Alice's young grandson, who had been with his mother in the living room, came into her bedroom to hear the chapter. It had been years since I had read Milne's book, and I doubt very much if I had understood it completely when I was a child. In it, Pooh learns that Christopher Robin will soon leave the Forest for what we adult readers know is boarding school. Both find saying goodbye very difficult, as we also found it hard to say goodbye to Alice that day. Christopher Robin begs Pooh never to forget him even if the boy lives to be a hundred and Pooh to be ninety-nine. Milne ends the book, saying, "So they went off together. But wherever they go, and whatever happens to them on the way, in that enchanted place on the top of the Forest, a little boy and his Bear will always be playing" ([1928] 1961, 179–80). Alice was not able to talk or respond, but we think she was hearing what we read. Under the circumstances, we all found the passage very moving.

In return for the time we spent with Alice, we received a lesson of amazing bravery in the face of incurable disease and certain death at a relatively young age. Her good humor and her delight when we read to her were infectious. The three of us who read to her became much closer to each other, as well as to her. After Alice died, her son Sam asked all three of us to speak at the memorial service. We joined many of her former colleagues from the Baltimore *Sun*, who spoke movingly about her earlier life and work. The service made a fitting end to Alice's productive life, but for us, the loss was more tangible. We all got such pleasure from reading aloud to her that we miss it very much.

In sum, I think that I have adjusted to the current situation, but I'm aware that in time new problems will emerge that may upset my equilibrium. Fortunately, being able to talk to friends who have had similar experiences is very helpful. I am hopeful that when more changes occur I will find support from the well-trained staff and my friends, but of course time will tell.

REFERENCES

Baltimore Sun. 2011. "How Snowmageddon 2010 Remains With Us Today." February 9. Accessed June 24, 2015. http://www.baltimoresun .com/news/maryland/bal-life-changing-snow-pg-photogallery.html.

Carrns, Ann. 2011. "The Company You Keep." Retirement, *New York Times*, September 15. Accessed 2011. http://www.nytimes. com/2011/09/16/businessretirementspecial/a-retirement-home-with-familiarneighbors.

Carson, Rachel. 1963. "Dear One." *Letters of Note Blog*, April 8, 2014. Accessed August 18, 2015. http://lettersofnote.tumblr.com/ post/82100183292/dear-one.

Clendinen, Dudley. 2008. *A Place Called Canterbury: Tales of the New Old Age in America*. New York: Viking.

Horner, Joyce. 1982. *That Time of Year: A Chronicle of Life in a Nursing Home*. Boston: University of Massachusetts Press.

Lear, Linda. 1997. *Rachel Carson: Witness for Nature*. New York: Henry Holt.

Milne, A. A. (1928) 1961. *The House at Pooh Corner*. New York: E. P. Dutton.

Pope, Elizabeth. 2011. "Coming Together to Make Aging a Little Easier." Retirement, *New York Times*, September 15. Accessed September 16, 2011. http://www.nytimes.com/2011/09/16/business/retirement special/caring-collaborative-members-look-out-for-each other.

Ray, Ruth E. 2008. *Endnotes: An Intimate Look at the End of Life*. New York: Columbia University Press.

Reimer, Susan. 2008. "The Middle Ages: Age-Old Problem: Parents' Care." *Baltimore Sun*, June 8. Accessed October 3, 2011. http://www .baltimoresun.com/entertainment/balalreimer08jun08, 0,7257648,print.

TWO

Coming to Care

Ruth Ray Karpen

In chapter 1, Anne Wyatt-Brown presents a compelling story about her struggles adjusting to life as a new resident in a continuing-care retirement community. As a narrative scholar and a feminist gerontologist, I am particularly interested in the questions her story raises about the ethics of care. Specifically, what does it mean to *care* (about ourselves and others) in old age? What constitutes a caring community, and how does one become a member? In the tradition of feminist ethicists Carol Gilligan (1993), Joan Tronto (1994), Eva Kittay (1999; Kittay and Felder 2002), and Margaret Urban Walker (2007), I think of care in terms of relationships, rather than abstract principles. To *care* means to make a moral decision to take responsibility for one's self and others and to act accordingly. Caring, in the words of Tronto, is "not simply a cerebral concern, or a character trait, but the concern of living, active humans engaged in the processes of everyday living. Care is both a practice and a disposition" (1994, 104). Tronto explains, following Nell Noddings (1984), that "semantically, care derives from an association with the notion of burden; to care implies more than simply a passing interest or fancy but instead the acceptance of some form of burden" (103).

I bring to this analysis my experience of having edited, with feminist gerontologist Toni Calasanti, a book about old-age care during the Great Depression, before the majority of Americans over the age of sixty had access to Social Security benefits, Medicare, and Medicaid (Ray and Calasanti 2011). We called the book *Nobody's Burden* because then, as now, older people did not want to burden their families with care responsibilities, even though they often could not take care of themselves. Many family members, out of work and facing the loss of their homes, did not have the resources to assume the burden of their elders' care, yet they were legally required to do so. In 1930s America, when families could not meet their filial responsibilities, elder members were often sent to the county poor house, also called the "work house," because residents who were able, regardless of age, were expected to work for their keep.

Americans are fortunate now to have a wider range of care options. The fact that Anne and her husband Bert had the resources to move into a continuing-care community designed to meet their current and future needs significantly lessens the individual, familial, and social burden of their old-age care. Anne and Bert did not have to worry, "What is to become of me?" as did many older Americans during the Great Depression. As retired professors who enjoyed the benefits of life-long health insurance and long-term retirement plans, Anne and Bert have had more and better care available to them than most elders during the Great Depression ever received or hoped to receive, including retired professionals, some of whom spent their final days in the poor house (Langlois and Durocher 2011). Today, Americans dread the nursing home, and for good reason, but it provides far better care than the county poorhouse ever did.

A FEMINIST EXPLANATION OF CARE

Tronto (1994) has formulated what is now a well-known paradigm for quality care in the twenty-first century. She proposes that care involves four key phases: *caring about*, which includes recognizing that care is necessary and determining that a specific need must be met; *taking care of*, which includes assuming responsibility for the identified need and deciding how to meet it; *care-giving*, which involves directly meeting the need through actions such as hands-on assistance; and *care receiving*, which involves responding to the care that has been given (105–7). Tronto suggests that we consider these related phases as an "ideal paradigm," something to aspire to as individuals and societies (109). All four phases must be present for genuine caring to occur in respectful and reciprocal relationships of caregivers and care receivers.

Anne's story can be read as an example of this caring process at the individual level. Her description makes clear that she *cares about* meeting her husband's needs, as well as her own, while they make the difficult transition from living at home to living among frail elders in a retirement community. She and Bert have *taken care of* their changing physical needs by researching their options, selling their home, selecting and moving into Roland Park Place, and making the effort to become socially integrated residents of this community.

Although she does not belabor the details, Anne is surely a *caregiver* to Bert, driving him to doctor appointments and assisting him with activities of daily living, and he no doubt gives care to her, as he is able and according to her needs. The important thing to remember about care—self-care and the care that others provide us—is that most of us take it for granted until we become disabled, which forces us into a state of awareness about the many forms of care we need on a daily basis. We may think of ourselves as "independent," but we are far more interdependent than we realize.

The success of the caring process that Anne and Bert went through in their transition to the retirement community depended on how well they could meet their needs in this new place. Here is where the dramatic conflict appears in Anne's story: She is not sure whether, in making the necessary move to meet Bert's physical needs, they can also meet their social needs. Anne is also concerned about finding the intellectual support that is vital to her own healthy aging. Friendship and stimulating conversation are important to her sense of well-being, as is the ability to use her knowledge as a gerontologist. Can she remain vibrant and active here, despite the ageist stereotypes imposed upon her from the outside? The subtext of this story, as with most stories of later life, revolves around the nature of change: How long will this period of independent living last for Anne and Bert? What new needs lie ahead? Anne writes that she sees "signs of the future every day that are painful, consisting of disability, decline, and death." But this foreboding is tempered by the recognition that she now belongs to a community of fellow retirees and professional caregivers who will help her adapt to whatever changes may come. One of the main social and emotional benefits of an age-segregated community such as Roland Park Place is the opportunity to share with and learn from others who are going through the same age-related experiences.

Anne's story recalls other important aspects of a feminist ethic of care. In explaining her shift from "merely observing the community" to "feeling a part of the group," Anne acknowledges the importance of moving from "outsider" to "insider" as a resident of Roland Park Place. Such a move requires both outer and inner change on her part. Outwardly, she made the physical move from the condominium on Stony Run Lane to Roland Park Place; inwardly, she is still learning to live with and accept others who are in various stages of mental and physical decline. Anne and Bert must learn to inhabit this new space emotionally and existentially.

Feminist ethicists suggest that, in order to move into the *emotional space* of a care community, one must embrace the experience and come to know the other residents, able and disabled, on their own terms. Philosopher Robin Fiore (1999) explains that such a move involves more than empathy or identifying with the other. It requires the recognition of the other's "unique particularity"; genuine care involves "apprehending the world from the other's reality and acting on the basis of the other's understanding of herself and her needs" (248). Such acts require higher levels of attentiveness, beginning first with a willingness to hold one's own fears and projections in check, followed by a willingness to make the effort to know another as she knows herself. These acts of caring, says Lustbader (1991), can revive and renew all people involved if they can learn to accept their differences without fear. Residents must also learn to grant illness, disability, and frailty their own validity, according to Lustbader. Rather than seeing only limitations, which is the view from outside the experience, caring participants who approach illness and frailty from inside the experience will find not only strengths but further possibilities for growth and development. Philosopher Sarah Ruddick (1999) reinforces this position by listing the potential "virtues" in frailty: accepting change and uncertainty with grace; showing genuine concern for others' frailties; acknowledging one's limitations and accepting help in ways that are gratifying to the helper; developing the capacity "to forgive and let go, to accept, adjust, and appreciate"; and learning to live and even thrive emotionally and spiritually in the face of one's own death (50).

These virtues, of course, occur in relations of care that involve moral and psychological struggle, as well as a tolerance for strong and ambivalent feelings. According to Ruddick, the virtues in old age "deal not only with conflicts of will but with efforts to live and care well" (1999, 58). In such cases, to "care well" requires engaging fully in the struggle and not turning away. Closing the gap between witness and participant requires proximity (Lustbader 1991, 52), which means that we must find the courage to "venture as far as we can into the territory of illness" (54). From this perspective, living at Roland Park Place provides Anne a unique opportunity. By sharing in the lived experience of dependency, Anne especially, as an able-bodied member of this community, stands to gain foreknowledge that could make her own final years less frightening and burdensome.

Anne's chapter title, "A Wife's Life, a Humanist's Journey," reveals a desire to use her knowledge as a particular *kind* of person in this community—as a caring wife *and* a humanistic scholar. In her efforts to become a caring member, Anne has been talking with others, participating in activities, listening, observing, reflecting, and considering her feelings. These are the methods of a phenomenologist who studies experience from the first-person point of view. Anne is doing what I have called "passionate scholarship" in gerontology, using her emotions as well as her intellect to explore a subject of deep personal interest (Ray 2008). Anne's story reflects an understanding of decline based on the experiences of her husband and other residents who are experiencing loss. Anne does not write from within the experience of disability herself. Indeed, she maintains a comfortable distance in regard to frailty, describing herself as "relatively young" in comparison to other residents, most of whom are "much older," and admitting an initial aversion to the lineup of walkers and wheelchairs in the common areas. Early in the story, she reveals a reluctance to get too close to the very frail members of this community. Yet she admires the kindness of other residents who "cheerfully eat with those who are in wheelchairs or have spotty memories," and later befriended "two people in wheelchairs" and now associates regularly with an old friend whose stroke inhibits her speech and who can no longer walk. In these gestures of friendship and community—these *relations* of care, as feminists describe them—Anne is getting closer to understanding what Thomas Cole and I have called "the existential marrow of aging and dying" (Cole and Ray 2010). Indeed, she is closer to understanding aging and dying than most gerontologists will ever get through their academic research and theorizing. She *cares* about aging and dying in a different way than she did when she was a gerontologist studying them from "outside" the experience.

One of the benefits of humanistic scholarship is that it allows researchers to *be human* in their work. In their explorations of life's mysteries—those questions that have no definitive answers—humanists are allowed to express their own confusion, frustration, anger, and despair. In her narrative, Anne reveals concerns about the future and her ambivalence about assuming the role of gerontologist at Roland Park Place. She wants to turn the occasion of her move into an opportunity to learn new things and perhaps teach others what she has learned, but initially she was not sure how to do this, as is evident in her other early remark that she "might study the inhabitants" of Roland Park Place as a researcher.

THE PERSONAL AS PROFESSIONAL

By offering her personal reflections on living in a care community, Anne now joins feminist scholars who have long claimed that scholarly writing should reflect the interrelationship of personal, political, and professional ways of knowing. They argue that we should not stand outside the issues in our field as dispassionate observers, personally untouched by them. Instead, it is "more human, more politic, more polite, more interesting, more accurate when we acknowledge the extent to which the examined object reflects the examining subject" (Freedman and Frey 2009, 4). Indeed, for many feminists, theorizing the personal is a "necessary corrective to pseudo-objectivity" (4). Gerontologist Ronald Manheimer (2009) agrees on philosophical grounds. He concludes that "once humanistic scholars enter the land of older people they are bound to encounter familiar faces—their own. That's when the fun begins. For here is a hermeneutic circle or set of concentric circles through which, by virtue of the scholar's own aging process, he or she moves ever closer to the center. As the scholar attempts a deeper understanding of what it means to grow old, he or she must struggle with the problem of finding a suitable framework—one that includes the student of ageing as well as the subjects" (284). In her story, Anne reveals her struggle to find a framework for making sense of her personal journey into the world of older people.

As a feminist gerontologist, I see that Anne is uniquely positioned to assume the archetypal role of the crone within the field of gerontology, as well as in her own life. The word *crone* derives from the word *crown* and represents a "crowning" of one's life experiences, a coming-into-one's own authority in later life. In contemporary societies, the crone is a universal symbol of maturity for men and women alike. In matriarchal societies, the crone represented development across the life course of women especially—the evolution of youth into old age, and a coming full circle at the end of life. As feminist historian Barbara Walker explains, the crone symbolizes becoming, not being, and reminds us that life is perpetual transition, "like a sunrise or sunset passing from darkness to light, and from light to darkness. . . . The Virgin [becomes] the Mother [becomes] the Crone," who represents the culmination of all that has gone before (1995, 29).

Just as important as her expression of the past is the crone's expression of the future. She reflects new images and meanings that are only possible *because* of what has gone before. As Walker notes, without this cyclic understanding of being and becoming, in cultures devoid of the crone archetype, neither men nor women will come into full maturity. They are perpetually stuck in youth (the virgin phase) or adulthood (the mother phase). The crone archetype, however, propels us forward individually and culturally by offering a powerful image of *becoming*, even in old age. She represents the end stage of our psychospiritual journey, a period of introspection, reflection, spiritual and existential growth, and the shedding of everything that lacks truth and meaning. The crone integrates all forms of intelligence—analytic, empathic, intuitive—to achieve this expanded awareness. Psychologist Jean Shinoda Bolen describes the crone as the "goddess of the crossroads," because she positions herself at the fork in the road, living in the present while looking backward and forward to the future (1994, 271). She forces us to make a conscious choice to move forward in one direction or another, prompting us to keep moving, even toward death, because that is the way of life. Anne's narrative, along with her epilogue, where she tells of Bert's death and her own health problems, shows us how one woman manages to keep looking ahead and moving forward, despite the challenges of later life and an unknown future.

Researching and writing from the position of the crone, as Anne is beginning to do, takes courage. But the payoff is greater wisdom and compassion for people of all ages. The crone can show us what it means to age with dignity and to care and be cared for in communities where old people truly matter.

REFERENCES

Bolen, Jean Shinoda. 1994. *Crossing to Avalon: A Woman's Midlife Pilgrimage*. San Francisco: Harper San Francisco.

Cole, Thomas R., and Ruth E. Ray. 2010. "The Humanistic Study of Aging Past and Present, or Why Gerontology Still Needs Interpretive Inquiry." In *A Guide to Humanistic Studies in Aging: What Does It Mean to Grow Old?*, edited by Thomas R. Cole, Ruth E. Ray, and Robert Kastenbaum, 1–29. Baltimore: Johns Hopkins University Press.

Fiore, Robin N. 1999. "Caring for Ourselves: Peer Care in Autonomous Aging." In *Mother Time: Women, Aging, and Ethics*, edited by Margaret M. Walker, 245–60. Lanham, MD: Rowman and Littlefield.

Freedman, Diane P., and Olivia Frey. 2009. "Self/Discipline: An Introduction." In *Autobiographical Writing across the Disciplines*, edited by Diane P. Freedman and Olivia Frey, 1–40. Durham, NC: Duke University Press.

Gilligan, Carol. 1993. *In a Different Voice: Psychological Theory and Women's Development*. Boston: Harvard University Press.

Kittay, Eva F. 1999. *Love's Labor: Essays on Women, Equality, and Dependency*. New York: Routledge.

Kittay, Eva F., and Ellen K. Felder, eds. 2002. *The Subject of Care: Feminist Perspectives on Dependency*. Lanham, MD: Rowman and Littlefield.

Langlois, Janet, and Mary E. Durocher. 2011. "The Haunting Fear: Narrative Burdens in the Great Depression." In *Nobody's Burden: Lessons from the Great Depression on the Struggle for Old-Age Security*, edited by Ruth E. Ray and Toni Calasanti, 245–71. Lanham, MD: Lexington Books.

Lustbader, Wendy. 1991. *Counting on Kindness: The Dilemmas of Dependency*. New York: Free Press.

Manheimer, Ronald J. 2009. "Gateways to Humanistic Gerontology." In *Valuing Older People: A Humanistic Approach to Ageing*, edited by Ricca Edmondson and Hans Joachim Von Kondratowitz, 284–87. Bristol, UK: Policy Press.

Noddings, Nel. 1984. *Caring: A Feminine Approach to Ethics and Moral Education*. Berkeley: University of California Press.

Ray, Ruth E. 2008. *Endnotes: An Intimate Look at the End of Life*. New York: Columbia University Press.

Ray, Ruth E., and Toni Calasanti, eds. 2011. *Nobody's Burden: Lessons from the Great Depression on the Struggle for Old-Age Security*. Lanham, MD: Lexington Books.

Ruddick, Sara. 1999. "Virtues and Age." In *Mother Time: Women, Aging, and Ethics*, edited by Margaret M. Walker, 45–60. Lanham, MD: Rowman and Littlefield.

Tronto, Joan. 1994. *Moral Boundaries: A Political Argument for an Ethic of Care*. New York: Routledge.

Walker, Barbara G. 1995. *The Crone: Woman of Age, Wisdom and Power*. San Francisco: Harper and Row.

Walker, Margaret Urban. 2007. *Moral Understandings: A Feminist Study in Ethics*. 2nd ed. New York: Oxford University Press.

THREE

Lifelong Strengths Ground Later-Life Wisdom

Helen Q. Kivnick

*Developing wisdom as we age toward later life requires surviv-*ing and incorporating life's tragedies, fully experiencing life's richest satisfactions, and carrying on daily life with integrity (Erikson, Erikson, and Kivnick 1986). In closely reading Anne's narrative, I realized that the psychosocial strengths that helped her adapt to the big move developed, as they do for all of us, through a lifetime of experience. But I also realized that I could not fully understand the role these strengths played in Anne's narrative without hearing more, in her own words, about her earlier life. So, over several telephone conversations, she told me decades of stories that helped explain more deeply what the move to Roland Park Place has meant to her and how she is using her core of accumulated strengths to create the new phase of her life she describes in her narrative. It became increasingly clear that Anne was "matured by culture" in ways that have provided invaluable resources for adapting to current relational, physical, and cultural challenges of aging.

Erik Erikson was an eminent twentieth-century psychoanalyst, psychologist, and life-cycle scholar. He is best known for originating today's generally accepted understanding of psychosocial development over the entire course of life, presented in *Childhood and Society* (1950), and for explicating the concept of an adolescent identity crisis, illustrated in his book *Young Man Luther* (1962). Erikson's way of looking at human lives integrates the influences of personality, history, and culture on the development of individual identity. With this lens, Erikson encourages the appropriate use of psychological and developmental constructs in our efforts to understand personal meaning and purpose in aging. His work encourages gerontologists to explore "the elusive, the awe inspiring, the disturbing... aspects of growing older" (Kivnick and Pruchno 2011, 145), as part of an overall effort to "address complex questions that have no definitive answers" (143).

So it is Erikson's thematic "virtues" that I use to characterize Anne's core strengths and to constitute the backbone of this chapter. These illustrate how the forging and renewing of psychosocial strengths permits us to meet life's successive challenges and opportunities. This process also illustrates one way developmental theory can enrich our understanding of Anne's life narrative—and our own, as well. Finally, noting these strengths across Anne's life illustrates how we can grow into old age with grace and resilience by appropriately exercising and renewing thematic strengths as each life stage requires.

Anne's first core strength, to use Erikson's terminology, is *competence*. From the time that she was a bookworm in elementary school, Anne excelled at reading, writing, and thinking. Also true to the related theme of industriousness, she developed capacities to plan, act, and, perhaps most important, to persevere.

Her second core strength is an inventive *purposefulness*. The very young Anne knew she was out of place in local schools; on her own, she devised and implemented a plan to go to boarding school after ninth grade. The adult Anne created a professional niche in the college composition world; she also fashioned a distinguished career as a literary gerontologist.

Love is a third domain of her strength. A product of a specific historical era, culture, and personality, Anne married her life to Bert Wyatt-Brown's in a way that a comparably accomplished woman ten or twenty years later might have had difficulty deciding to do. From their first meeting, Anne and Bert became intellectual partners. Sometimes they collaborated on work. More often, they contributed to each other's disparate projects, enriching each other's intellectual development and ever deepening the layers of their intimacy.

Care stands out as Anne's fourth Eriksonian strength, best understood as the product of an important balance between putting oneself second in the service of caring for a relatively weaker other, on the one hand, and providing comparably loving care for oneself, on the other hand. This strength recalls Ruth Ray Karpen's earlier discussion of a feminist ethic of care. As a scholar, Anne learned early to care for ideas and intellectual products. To that capacity she added caring for the marriage and family that became the center of her adult life. These were the figure, so to speak, set within the ground of her scholarly world. Early in Anne and Bert's marriage, family included their first daughter Laura, for whom Anne provided loving care through the little girl's prolonged, heartbreaking terminal illness. On the heels of Laura's death, Anne, in quick succession, completed a dissertation, and then shifted to full-time nurturing of her traumatized younger daughter, Natalie. Fast forward to mid-career when Bert's recurring medical needs called for her ongoing—though intermittent—care in response to a series of crises.

Anne has spent a lifetime vitally involved with the life of the mind—shared with her scholar-husband and sculpted around the dailiness of their two careers and family household.[1] Anne's scholarly world involved English literature, women's writing, and writers' insights about aging. She has also spent a lifetime purposefully enacting loving care for family, students, and disciplines in ways that add depth to her insights on literary gerontology. I share the following abridged life history to help readers contextualize Anne's strengths, as they have come to the fore during her big move.

A BRIEF BIOGRAPHY OF ANNE WYATT-BROWN

Raised in Baltimore and schooled in an atmosphere of propriety, Anne came of age in an era when it was far more typical for a highly educated woman to build a career around her husband's academic positions than to optimize her own academic success. She had always been fascinated by the writings of E. M. Forster. After graduating from Radcliffe in 1961, she was visiting her family in Baltimore when she met a Johns Hopkins graduate student at a party. Someone told her that Bert, the tall man across the room, had known Forster. She introduced herself, and it seems they were soul mates ever after. From the beginning they were intellectual partners, delighting in one another's curiosities and talents. They shared scholarly passions, respect for each other's ideas, and family backgrounds of mannered Southern propriety.

Anne did a master's degree in teaching while Bert finished his history thesis. In the fall of 1962, they made the first of what would ultimately be ten cross-country family moves around his academic life. Anne taught freshman composition, creative writing, and Great Books while they were in Colorado, where Laura was born. From Bert's first academic position, Anne's own scholarship flourished largely outside university responsibilities, but it was never outside her many-layered relationship with Bert. Neither was her care for home and beloved family members.

When they moved to Cleveland in 1966, Anne began a PhD in English Literature at Case Western Reserve. Shortly after their arrival in Cleveland, Laura was diagnosed with neurofibromatosis, an incurable condition in which inoperable brain tumors cause seizures and interfere with normal development. Their second daughter, Natalie, was born before Anne finished her degree. Natalie was not yet two when Laura, then seven, died. That was a tough year for all three remaining family members. In 1972, Anne finished her degree, and she stayed at home the following year, trying to heal herself and create stability and predictability for then-four-year-old Natalie.

When Anne returned to work, it was to teach freshman English at the Cleveland Institute of Art. Although her subject was literature, Anne had discovered that she had a gift for teaching students to write, and she had an affinity for academically challenged college students. Soon her literature courses became classes in writing, and they attracted not only freshmen, but also older students who needed help. For nine years, she worked with students who came to her not knowing that they had any ideas or knowledge worth putting on paper. In her classes, they found a voice. Anne was developing a new niche for herself, as well.

Outside her classroom, the field of gerontology was beginning to resonate in the Humanities and the Arts. While attending a Humanities in Aging conference, Anne discovered Barbara Pym's 1977 retirement novel *Quartet in Autumn*. Proposing to research Pym's novel, Anne became a fellow with the National Endowment for the Humanities in the emerging area of "old age in history and literature." The Wyatt-Browns moved to Florida in 1983. That same year, Anne joined the Gerontological Society of America and immediately became a stalwart of the Humanities and Arts Committee.

The University of Florida needed a program to teach writing to graduate students we would now call English as a Second Language learners or ESL. Anne was an expert in this area. Through the Linguistics Department, she taught these students until they were competent to meet college writing requirements. She started a second program to train graduate Linguistics students to teach writing to their ESL classmates. She continued to nurture her gerontological humanities scholarship outside her formal job.

Anne was doing research in England for her book on Barbara Pym (Wyatt-Brown 1992) when, in 1986, Bert was diagnosed with atrial fibrillation. He was then fifty-four. This diagnosis marked the onset of a series of major medical incidents for him, including six bouts of bladder cancer between 1994 and 2003, and a triple-bypass and valve repair surgery in 2001. As she describes it with well-practiced mastery, only the heart condition involved major surgery and rehabilitation. But cumulatively, these episodes repeatedly intruded Anne and

Bert's own mortality into their middle-adult life. In addition, Bert's bouts of illness likely directed Anne's vital involvements toward caring for and supporting him, at precisely that time in her life when she had anticipated concentrating on her own scholarly development. Nevertheless, she proposed a series in Age Studies to the University of Virginia Press, and she saw several books in that series through to publication, including her own coedited (with Janice Rossen)volume, *Aging and Gender in Literature: Studies in Creativity* (1993), Margaret Gullette's *Declining to Decline* (1997), and Ruth Ray's *Beyond Nostalgia: Aging and Life Story Writing* (2000).

BUILDING ON PAST STRENGTHS

The Wyatt-Browns both retired in 2004. Bert was seventy-two, had just survived his sixth bout of bladder cancer, and was becoming suspicious about his increasing shortness of breath. Anne was sixty-five. Since her years in gerontology had familiarized her with important considerations about retirement, they had planned well for this major change. They knew that they wanted to leave Florida. They knew they wanted to live near other academics and humanists, preferably near a good university. They liked the East Coast. Unexpectedly, Anne's sister announced that she had decided to sell her home in Baltimore. It was near academics, humanists, and a good university. The house was appealing, affordable, and in a neighborhood where they wanted to live. They seized the opportunity.

For Anne, this was a return to the hometown she had left when she started boarding school in Massachusetts, back in the ninth grade. This return and Anne's retirement coincided with her appointment as the founding coeditor of the newly established *Journal of Aging and Humanities* (*JAHA*). She held this position through December 2010, when the journal folded. Earlier, she had been guest editor of the *Generations* issue "Listening to Older People's Stories," published in 2003.

The couple's move to Baltimore was a good one. The city, the neighborhood, the home were all familiar and desirable. Anne's sister recommended a nearby church; Anne and Bert tried it and felt quickly at home. The church was friendly to children, providing a lively counterpoint to the quiet ideas that so deeply engaged them. And the church choir was "good— but not so good that we couldn't participate," says Anne. (In addition to her job, scholarship, and family involvement, choral singing had been a lifelong pleasure since her boarding school days.) The Wyatt-Browns attended choir rehearsals together for more than a year, while Bert's lungs could still support his singing.

Anne has woven her signature strengths into a sturdy fabric of life. Outside a family life of caring she managed to create and nurture two separate professional careers. Around Bert's academic positions, she fashioned a job of teaching English and writing to "nontraditional" students. And around that job she created and sustained a life of scholarship (significantly through the Gerontological Society of America), finding intellectual colleagues nationally and internationally.

Anne's years of researching and writing in gerontology provided a solid foundation for the Wyatt-Browns' retirement planning. And when Bert's pulmonary fibrosis interacted with a 2010 snowstorm to constitute a new crisis that required immediate action, Anne had already accumulated the necessary information (the right retirement community, admission application materials) and could ground it in the personal strengths and skills (competence, love, care, and purpose) required to respond effectively. Anne describes the move to Roland Park Place as prompted by circumstances beyond their control, that is, an unnavigable snowstorm. Catalyst notwithstanding, she very much took control of the move itself—using the same psychosocial strengths that had given shape to her personal, lifelong pattern of vital involvement.

Anne has continued to use these same strengths, this same pattern of deeply meaningful involvement, to move from being, initially, an observer at Roland Park Place to becoming a creator of her and Bert's engaged life there, and, more recently, to becoming a valued community participant in her own right. They had chosen a residential community where their neighbors would be scholars, artists, and humanists, like themselves. At Roland Park Place, they believed they would be likely to find people who could become real friends and to experience a community that was already functioning effectively to support the kinds of activities, occupations, recreations, and productive pursuits that had always been most meaningful to the two of them.

Moving households around jobs, as Anne and Bert had done all their lives, requires specific skills and the ability to use time and energy wisely. In people with appropriate internal strengths, frequent moving can support adaptation. However, later-life moves around disabilities are potentially much more difficult. Daily needs. Daily limits. Daily pains. Daily fears and accumulating regrets. Yet Anne's interwoven strengths of competence, inventive purpose, love, and care enabled her to create a life structure in Roland Park Place that supports ongoing, multifaceted engagement for both herself and Bert.

They chose a two-bedroom apartment, where one of the bedrooms could serve as the study that Bert required to continue his research, and where Anne could create her own work space in another room. As they had always done, they worked on their own projects, and they contributed to each other's. Anne edited the last issues of *JAHA* from her Roland Park Place work space. She now helps edit the Roland Park Place literary review. She attends an in-house poetry class that broadens her literary horizons; while Anne studied and taught poetry almost entirely from England, the community poetry teacher specializes in recent American literature.

The Wyatt-Browns always exercised together. Although Bert's participation diminished due to ill health, Anne continues to take exercise classes at Roland Park Place and to work independently with two different trainers. She serves on the community's fitness committee. And she is forging satisfying friendships with Roland Park Place neighbors who, like her, create intimacy through literature and through purposeful accomplishment. Anne's current involvements renew her lifelong strength of *generativity*, which Erikson described as the striving to create or nurture things that would benefit society and future generations. She serves on committees, helps edit publications, works on producing dramatic readings, and provides personal support to the people who are becoming her new close friends. Exemplifying the reciprocity of vital involvement, Anne also *receives* support and draws strength from each of these caring, meaningful engagements. Indeed, the very act of sharing her story here and prompting thoughtful, written responses from her colleagues in gerontology illustrates an additional expression of reciprocal generativity.

In Anne's monthly caregiver group, attended mostly by people who care for partners with dementia, the group associates Anne's "outsider" status as a gerontologist with valuable expertise. She can laugh with the others at now-past stories of their spouses escaping from Roland Park Place. Along with the rest of them, she knows that these events were far from funny while they were happening and that laughing about them now asserts some mastery over the terror. Anne, the editor of "Listening to Other People's Stories," well knows that sharing stories is a way to create solidarity. She offers practical suggestions for problems that are, for the others, so emotionally fraught that even obvious solutions may seem elusive. (Roland Park Place now posts near the front desk photos of residents who are known to wander so that receptionists pay attention when these individuals walk out unattended.) Unusual among continuous care communities, the administration prioritizes residents' everyday sense of home over the fear for safety that leads similar communities to confine "wanderers" to locked floors.

With lessons learned from new friends, Anne is continuing to strengthen the "anticipatory mastery" of age-related psychosocial challenges that are likely to arise in her future. We are all likely to need such anticipatory mastery—if we are lucky enough to live long enough, with partners that we love enough. She is certainly taking advantage of many aspects of what the Roland Park Place environment offers. And, in the familiar reciprocal pattern of vital involvement, she is contributing to what that same environment *has* to offer—to herself and all other residents.

I don't want to sugarcoat Anne and Bert's life—or the challenges of aging, in general. I don't want to trivialize the initial shock of a life surrounded by people who look like your great-grandparents did, even as you may look—to younger people—very much the same way. And I certainly don't mean to gloss over the physical and emotional pains of caring for a lifelong partner who you know will not recover. But I do want to celebrate the new expressions of strength, mastery, inventiveness, love, and care that can emerge in a later life well anticipated and wisely lived.

We all know that pains of loss are part of life. And those of us over fifty have all experienced enough anticipatory twinges of these pains to guess we won't be spared increasing losses in years to come. As gerontologists, we also know that we grow into old age with our own personal life core of accumulated strengths and limitations. Indeed, when aging poses so very many challenges to our sense of self, exercising and renewing core psychosocial strengths—as Anne is doing—remains the one reliable basis for optimizing continuity.

In some ways, the ability to cope with new pains and challenges is, in and of itself, a kind of triumph. In other ways, this coping is a source of new and renewed inner strength. As Anne's adjustment to Roland Park Place illustrates, we can each build on the life core of our accumulated strengths. And we can maintain the vital involvement that has always enabled us to draw support *from* the environment, to create meaning in ourselves, and to contribute strength back *to* the environment that must continue to sustain us all.

REFERENCES

Erikson, Erik H. 1950. *Childhood and Society.* New York: W. W. Norton.

———. 1962. *Young Man Luther: A Study in Psychoanalysis and History.* New York: W. W. Norton.

Erikson, Erik H., Joan M. Erikson, and Helen Q. Kivnick. 1986. *Vital Involvement in Old Age.* New York: W. W. Norton.

Gullette, Margaret Morganroth. 1997. *Declining to Decline: Cultural Combat and the Politics of the Midlife.* Charlottesville: University Press of Virginia.

Kivnick, Helen Q. 2010. "Dancing Vital Involvement: A Creative Old Age." *Journal of Aging, Humanities and the Arts* 4 (4): 421–30.

Kivnick, Helen Q., and Shirley V. Murray. 1997. "Vital Involvement: An Overlooked Source of Identity in Frail Elders." *Journal of Aging and Identity* 2 (3): 205–23.

Kivnick, Helen Q., and Rachel Pruchno. 2011. "Bridges and Boundaries: Humanities and Arts Enhance Gerontology." *Gerontologist* 51 (2): 142–44. doi: 10.1093/geront/gnr007.

Kivnick, Helen Q., and Courtney K. Wells. 2014. "Untapped Richness in Erik H. Erikson's Rootstock." *Gerontologist* 54 (1): 40–50. doi: 10.1093/geront/gnt123.

Ray, Ruth. 2000. *Beyond Nostalgia: Aging and Life Story Writing.* Charlottesville, University Press of Virginia.

Wyatt-Brown, Anne. 1992. *Barbara Pym: A Critical Biography.* University of Missouri Press.

Wyatt-Brown, Anne, and Janice Rossen, eds. 1993. *Aging and Gender in Literature: Studies in Creativity.* Charlottesville: University Press of Virginia.

This work was partially supported by the USDA National Institute of Food and Agriculture, Hatch project MIN-55-035.

1. *Vital involvement* has been defined as personally meaningful, reciprocally influential engagement with the world outside the self (Erikson et al. 1986; Kivnick and Murray 1997; Kivnick 2010; Kivnick and Wells 2014).

AFTERWORD

Making Oneself at Home

Margaret Morganroth Gullette

Anne Wyatt-Brown's account—the heart of this book—is absorbing both because she dared to tell it at all and because she tells it so honestly. She and her celebrated husband, the historian Bert Wyatt-Brown, moved into Roland Park Place, a large nearby continuing-care retirement community (CCRC) because of his health issues. She had none. It's a common situation—where people in long-term relationships come to have very different (and potentially competing) needs and have to make hard choices. Theirs were made suddenly. Anne was living in good health, without incident, at only seventy-one. Bert had a crisis. Moving into a community of mostly disabled and chronically ill people who were on average much older forced her suddenly to confront what being aged by culture means when she was not herself on the cusp of old age. She faced the risks of stigma by association. And the stigma is grave. Aversion toward old people, coupled with aversion to the frail or chronically ill or terminally ill—these are facts of aging-past-midlife, and of politicized ageism, and the fear of cognitive impairment, in the much-touted era of the New Longevity. Think of ageism as a risk of aging, similar to, say, osteoporosis but more common.

We know that people constitute their identities through narrative. But how they do it, ah, that's what matters. Anne might have told her story as a psychological decline, full of sensational material from the master narrative of old age, dramatizing Bert's crisis, ageist behaviors toward her, any personal depression. She didn't. The story she tells—how she coped—is told with composure. Yet the detail that it provides nevertheless has an unexpected power to shock.

My recognizing its power says more about my initial subjective attitude toward old age and disability than about Anne's experiences. Those who possess the superiority of health may willingly remain ignorant until we are rudely forced up against our need to know. I confess I was the same, despite two decades of research in age studies, until not very long ago.

For five years during my mother's nineties, I visited her when she was living in a retirement community nearby, where we ate meals with many coresidents, worked out on the machines, and socialized in activities, but where I had never needed to imagine myself as a resident. Frankly, I originally thought something like "inmate," even though the place was elegant, expensive for those who weren't on "scholarship," and filled with conversable knowledge workers from institutions such as Harvard and MIT as well as teachers, a pianist, a libararian, a poet. I talked to numerous newcomers as they arrived because my gregarious mother constituted herself a welcoming committee. I always joined her in praising the place. Conscious of myself as a younger person, I relished my differences—no doubt about it: my ability to walk tall, speak with cognitive confidence, be kind to the coresidents, and leave at the end of the visit. I was safe, a visitor. (Anne's openness encourages this confession.) Every single one of the newcomers told us how wrenching the move was, how beautiful their original home had been, how sad it made them to be in this place despite its hotel-like amenities. A few hinted that the move had lowered them in their own estimation. It took some people years to adjust. My mother's form of adjustment was to rebuild a social life, reinstitute her pleasures, grieve for her own losses, and praise the Homes, simultaneously.

Told too soon, these later-life stories could be painful, self-pitying, or tragic about strong-willed people felled by necessity and unable to change. These common tropes of identity loss and heartbreak, Anne utterly avoids. She waited until she had lived at Roland Park Place for two years before she looked back. She touches on the original hauteur of health, but not on her own grief or loss, suggesting she had no such feelings. No one who lives inside can afford to emphasize difference long. Anne may be reticent or stoic, I don't know, and she admits to ambivalence. But she is blessedly neither despairing nor chipper. I suspect she is simply a nicer person than I was, and better trained as a gerontologist.

She recognized none of Bert's needs as "competing" with her own; she simply moved into Roland Park Place, in her practical, no-nonsense way, and made it her home. She liked it, and she still likes it. Tactfully, she respects Bert's privacy and leaves his feelings unknown. So this is *her* story. As she tells it, she turns outward toward the other residents. "It didn't take too long before I stopped merely observing the community and began feeling a part of the group." In other words, she became the sort of anthropologist who goes native—a sensible outsider (capable of being politically incorrect) who becomes a sensitive insider, eschewing theory in favor of sharing her experiences. Ruth Ray Karpen, a feminist gerontologist, commenting on the essay, discusses the value of Anne's showing how this transformation occurred. And Helen Kivnick, a social psychologist writing from a life-course perspective, describes the qualities Anne had developed starting in childhood that enabled her to respond so well.

Fortunately, Anne's good will, knowledge of ageism, and steady self-awareness taught her pretty quickly what many of us, oddly enough, don't care to know in advance about such institutions: that people stay human, even in old age, even in wheelchairs and after strokes. Ray Karpen, who is the author of the remarkable memoir, *Endnotes* (under the name Ruth Ray [2008]), observes that learning this truth "requires a high level of attentiveness, an ability to hold one's own fears and projections in check." By making friends, trusting she would encounter equals, Anne's trust was confirmed.

Roland Park Place provides Anne with too many stories to generalize. One man who moved in because of his wife's health does voice regrets. People inside do suffer from ageism, Anne lets us know. Some residents feel humiliated when a friend on the outside asks whether they still drive. "Probably those people are scared of what the future might hold for them," Anne surmises. "They fear being forced to confront images of their future." By now the phrase "on the outside" conveys the "friend's" sense of otherness, not Anne's. The residents act in plays, exercise in the pool, go on trips. They live. And some die. Daringly, Anne tells of befriending another writer named

Alice, who is living-with-dying. This is the way a good narrative works: we are willing to get closer to the Other in order to follow the narrator's story wherever her life takes her.

There isn't finally an "inside" and an "outside." This place is as much a "community" as any neighborhood, and Anne remains a "community-dwelling" person, thank you very much. One point of calling it a community is that it provides solidarity close to home. Posh Roland Park Place is not one of the dreaded establishments that the term *nursing home* conjures up, but nursing homes too can provide the sociability that people living alone may crave without knowing it. In Louise Erdrich's (2008) *Plague of Doves*, Antone's ailing mother is said to be "anxious and ready to die." She may even have thrown herself down her basement stairs to hasten the end. When moved to the retirement home, she barks, "This is not what I had in mind!" But "It was surprising how quickly she got used to the place." She made a friend, played cards, shared TV shows, gained a few pounds, got her hair done. Antone says, "I had forgotten how social she was before her decline."

Many people are sure they will be miserable leaving homes they have been familiar with for so long, and they convince themselves they won't have to leave. "The home care revolution—a national move toward letting frail elders remain in their homes without resorting to residential facilities—is already under way, with more than half of America's direct-care workers engaged in a new form of the old-fashioned house call" (Peters 2013). There may be robots in some people's futures.

But even if people don't require live support for cooking meals or getting into a shower, solitude is sometimes a serious problem for those who choose to age in place. Home can be the place that isolates you from the world, where you lie in bed in a droopy slip. Several of the novels I describe later, tell stories of people like Antone's mother who grow happier, and even healthier, after making their big move. For Cecilia Condit, director of the film *Oh Rapunzel*, the image of her mother, formerly lethargic, but now nicely dressed and careering around the corridors on her motorized scooter, is a sign of independence and gaiety. As families have gotten smaller, and more and more adult children spread out globally, assisted-living residences or continuing-care communities may come to be seen as ideal, if only they can be made affordable.

Architecture—not space in some abstract theoretical way, but design—plays a huge mostly unseen role in social relations. (The field that focuses on such issues is called "architectural psychology," bless it.) Roland Park Place is designed, architecturally, to treat as equals people whose health worsens. About one woman who needs assistance, Anne notes that, because health care and independent living sections are in the same building, many of her friends have continued to visit her. Another CCRC I visited, however, had an architectural plan that isolates and demeans: one side had luxurious apartments, but across the parking lot a hidden area contained the wards. We can't care for people we don't see, and meet, and continue to know. The main point of "continuing care" is that those who live in such a residence keep the conversations going, as long as they can. They enjoy concerts, lectures, bingo sessions—whatever range of activities the community provides. In another exciting revolution that really does deserve the label *revolutionary*—that of *person-centered care*—people with cognitive impairments, even if they don't converse much, are provided with occasions to participate pleasurably with everyone else in the community in choral singing, art-making, theater, dance.

Anne provides some, just enough, institutional history—given through the experiences of people she knows. She tells about two aunts who had made similar moves and "were pleased with their choices." Anne's gaze is like the theatrical light called Lekos, bright and focused. A spot. She contextualizes her whole story in deft ways that skilled readers of memoir or fiction can appreciate.

The name CCRC is unwieldy: such care communities should find another kindlier name. (In Holland, they call them "Apartments for Life" [Rengier 2012]). To age in place and then to die in place—as Anne's friend Alice did—with comfort care, surrounded by caregivers who know you, and with friends of your own age by your side, sounds like an old-fashioned luxury. Nowadays, to come true, it requires new institutions with new financial products. Anne's stories have in fact made me rethink my own unexamined determination to stay unto death in my high-maintenance two-story Victorian house. I can now imagine circumstances in which a CCRC might be not just "the best available," a weak recommendation, but a good choice.

Even though Anne's account is not sociological, she touches on class issues. Roland Park Place (like her aunts' residences, like my mother's) is expensive. So is long-term care at home, except for that given by daughters and sons and other relatives. Both are out of reach for most Americans. Medicaid reimbursements in many states have been dropping for nursing homes, and many are being forced to close. Long-term care insurance was supposed to be included in the Affordable Care Act, but Health and Human Services quietly eliminated it, as resistance to the act grew. People who want such insurance policies—many fearing cognitive impairment or Alzheimer's long before they have any symptoms—are dependent on private insurers who charge high premiums. By 2020, Health and Human Services Secretary Kathleen Sebelius anticipates, "an estimated 15 million Americans will need some kind of long-term care and fewer than three percent have a long-term care policy" (2011).

Anne's memoir speaks from the inside of a potentially estranging experience in a way that makes it familiar, and bearable, and indeed acceptable, and, in the reader's imagination, livable. For such reasons, it seems to be—and Ruth and Helen agree—a landmark in this kind of narrative.

I am impressed by the diversity of my colleagues' approaches. I have given my say as to what Anne accomplished as a thinker and storyteller. Ruth expands in her sensitive way on the feminist philosophy of "caring." Helen tells us on the basis of an oral history how Anne's capabilities developed. Helen's was the original concept, of enriching Anne's experiential essay with interdisciplinary perspectives (critical age studies, biography, and analysis of psychological development). That has proved itself. We are all delighted to provide these decorative frames for Anne's big, intimate picture.

No doubt in time others will write many similar stories, eventually for the popular press. (I dread exposes like "I Lived for Sixty Days in a Nursing Home!" or a story like Anne's under a different title—"Old Like Me: Disguised as an Old Woman, Author Feels Disgust.") Future authors may not be able to handle this material with the frankness and mindfulness that Anne's plainspoken tale displays. Memoir, like fiction, gets us to live inside the head of "someone like us" in order to understand experiences that are beyond our normal ken. Political narratives, like the movies *Missing* and *Z*, take us to distant locations like Chile or Greece in turmoil. But places quite close to home can feel foreign—*unheimlich*. Nonfiction memoir—when it can avoid the expectable arc of frightening dramatization and hideous anticipations of decline—may have equivalent power to hold our attention, normalizing its characters' complex feelings amid their new locales.

Eventually, it may seem perplexing that in the early twenty-first century a book such as ours seemed essential to write. We may all hope that "eventual" day comes quickly.

Old age is not another country. Nor, more to the point here, is living-with-disability, or living-with-dying. Helen offers the term *anticipatory mastery* about willingly picking up knowledge and stories of later life that may help us all live better, longer. Many of us in the midlife cohorts are stubbornly behaving as if we could remain outsiders forever. I can't help recalling Ian, a character in Anne Tyler's 1991 novel, *Saint Maybe*. A man of scarcely forty, Ian suddenly feels in a bar that "he was very likely the oldest person present": "He looked down at the hand encircling his glass—the grainy skin on his knuckles, the gnarled veins in his forearm. How could he have assumed that old people were born that way? That age was an individual trait, like freckles or blond hair, that would never happen to him?" The sooner we figure out *how to be old*, wisely and kindly, as life changes us, the better off American society will be. This is precious knowledge in the era of the New Longevity.

Condit, Cecelia. *Oh, Rapunzel*. Accessed June 22, 2015. Excerpt at https://www.youtube.com/watch?v=LzqtooUFV7I.

Erdrich, Louise. 2008. *Plague of Doves*. New York: Harper Collins.

Peters, Barbara Smith. 2013. "The Home Care Revolution: Robots and Eldercare's Future." *Sarasota Herald Tribune/New America Media*, June 3. Accessed June 22, 2015. http://newamericamedia .org/2013/06/the-home-care-revolution-robots-and-elder cares-future.php.

Ray, Ruth. 2008. *Endnotes: An Intimate Look at the End of Life*. New York: Columbia University Press.

Rengier, Victor. 2012. "Going Dutch: A Mixed-Use Housing Model from the Netherlands Responds to the Aging Demographic." *Aging Today*, 33 (4, July/August). Accessed June 22, 2015. http://www.asaging.org/blog/going-dutch-mixed-use-housing-model-netherlands-responds-aging-demographic/.

Sebelius, Kathleen. 2011. "Secretary Sebelius Letter to Congress about CLASS." October 14. Accessed June 22, 2015. http://www.ltcconsultants.com/articles/2011/class-dismissed/ Sebelius-CLASS-Letter.pdf.

Tyler, Anne. 1991. *Saint Maybe*. New York: Knopf.

EPILOGUE

Still on the Journey, 2012–2015

2012–2015

Anne M. Wyatt-Brown

When I wrote the final version of my chapter on our transition to Roland Park Place, I knew that Bert would die fairly soon. Still, I had no idea when that would be and what those final days would be like. As it happened, he died November 5, 2012, in hospice at Roland Park Place, after only a very short time in the health care section of the building where the nurses could keep an eye on him.

The year 2012 was one marked by Bert's steady decline. We began to skip conferences that we had attended frequently in the past. Bert concentrated on composing the draft of the book he had started about the time we moved to Roland Park Place in 2010. He completed it in June and submitted it to Richard Holway of the University of Virginia Press. The press accepted the book, so the next few months were a race against time.

Bert worked very hard on the manuscript trying to answer the questions raised by the copy editor. Unfortunately, we had given away some of his books in order to fit into our apartment, which had less room for bookshelves than our house had. As a result, he couldn't find some of the citations that he needed. Nonetheless, having the manuscript to work on was a blessing. It kept him busy on the computer and happy to be productive. I was grateful that the work kept him safe so that I could continue doing the activities that gave me pleasure.

My sister, Susan Marbury, helped him try to answer the questions of the copy editor. As a result, she knew what Bert was thinking when he mulled over the requests for clarity. Her knowledge turned out to be a great help when the two of us later had to finish responding to the editor alone, finding answers to the queries that had baffled Bert.

When it was time in June for my fifty-fifth reunion from boarding school, I flew to Boston by myself. The year before, Bert and I had gone to my fiftieth college reunion, but it became apparent that he would have a difficult time at my school. None of the buildings had access for people in wheelchairs, and he would have been miserable the entire weekend. Instead, he stayed at Roland Park Place working on the book and eating dinner with several of our friends. At the end of the month when we had our fiftieth wedding anniversary, festivities with the family were reduced because of a power outage at Roland Park Place.

We went to Maine as usual that summer, driven by our daughter Natalie. This time the trip was complicated by problems suffered by both of us. I had sciatica, which caused a lot of pain in my back. I lay down on the back seat of the car to reduce the misery. Moreover, we discovered that Bert was tied to his oxygen much more completely than we had realized. On July 4, when we went out to dinner with friends, the battery for the oxygen tank stopped working. Bert immediately began to lose oxygenation. His level dropped into the 70s. Natalie insisted that we go to the hospital for treatment. As soon as Bert was put on a stable source of oxygen, his level went back to a normal range. I wanted to take him back to the cottage immediately, but Natalie thought he needed to be hospitalized. After several hours of waiting, we were released by the doctor. We realized then that Bert could not leave the cottage for any length of time except in the car where we could plug in the oxygen tank. Upon our return to Baltimore, I had surgery on my back on July 31. I quickly learned that Bert was not able to help me with any domestic chores, but somehow we survived.

In August, we went to see Bert's pulmonologist and told her of our problems in Maine. She insisted that we get hold of hospice, which we did. Six days later, a woman from hospice came to evaluate Bert. When she found out that he was writing a book, she worried that he was not eligible for hospice services. The doctor who was in charge, however, disagreed when he found out that Bert's oxygen had dropped into the 70s shortly after the battery failed. The next day, we had visits from a nurse and a social worker, and the following day, the Roman Catholic priest from hospice arrived. We enjoyed talking politics with him as it was an election year.

A month later, Hal Hajek, the dean from the Episcopal cathedral, came to discuss possible funeral services for both of us. That way, he confided in me, Bert would not feel singled out. We had a great time picking hymns, prayers, and anthems for our services. I insisted on hymns for me that had been favorites of mine at school, even though they had been removed from the revised hymnal. After Hal's visit, I continued to attend the caregiver support group at Roland Park Place because

I still found it helpful. I had met many other residents who were taking care of spouses, whose stories were much more traumatic than mine. I hoped to be able to imitate their sense of humor and resilience.

In October, Natalie visited for a few days, in order to have some quality time with her father. Her timing was excellent, and we all enjoyed each other's company. She tried to reorganize my desk, but that of course that turned out to be a hopeless task. After her visit, Bert and Susan continued to work on the book as much as possible. Bert went to some of the exercise classes at the fitness center, including one the week before he died.

On November 2, Bert fell, but he was able to roll forward and get up by himself. Susan came, and they continued their work. Susan also arrived at noon the next day, November 3, and the two of them completed the work that Bert was able to do. He approved an introduction that the copy editor wanted, but shortly thereafter he had another fall from which he could not get up. When the nurse arrived to see what was going on, she decided that he belonged in the health care center because he was coming to the end. We all knew that it was just a matter of time.

On November 4, friends sat with me at Bert's bedside in the nursing facility. That afternoon, Hal Hajek came to give Bert communion. He took one look at him and cut back the service drastically. He asked Bert to recite the Lord's Prayer and then gave him communion. That evening, a friend and I watched "Call the Midwife" in Bert's room—a program that both of us had watched with great pleasure in the past—and at 12:15 early the next morning he died. Two days after Bert's death, I attended my last caregivers' support group and told everyone what had happened. Bert was cremated, and we had the funeral service November 16 with Natalie and her family, as well as many of Bert's friends. The choir sang Bert's favorite anthem, and Hal preached a wonderful homily.

I found two things especially helpful in the time immediately after Bert's death. Being in the choir kept me busy. I attended many diocesan services and benefitted from the distraction. Besides choir, I was grateful for my friends and acquaintances at Roland Park Place. The residents and the staff were very supportive. I had many more dinner engagements than usual and was delighted to eat with so many different people. I went to the fitness center regularly and kept up my exercise routine. Getting out, talking with other people, and taking care of myself helped me cope with the loss.

Several things happened to me subsequently that made me realize how the move to Roland Park Place had been in my best interest as well as Bert's. In 2013, I had pneumonia twice, a circumstance that was unusual for me. The first time occurred when I was supposed to fly to Gainesville for a memorial gathering for Bert. Our friends postponed the gathering, and I was able to attend in March instead of January. I then had pneumonia once more in 2013 and later in 2014. Both times it was helpful being in a place where my dinner was provided, and I was surrounded by caring friends.

After Bert's death, Susan and I worked hard to see his book through press. I felt triumphant when friends at Johns Hopkins University were able to provide necessary citations that I could not have found on my own. Susan and I finished the index in the fall of 2013, and Bert's final book, *A Warring*

Nation: Honor, Race, and Humiliation in America and Abroad, was published in 2014. Susan and I were especially proud of that accomplishment.

Again the unexpected happened in 2014. I was diagnosed with breast cancer on January 29. Being at Roland Park Place so near to my family turned out to be a blessing. Because the cancer was aggressive, I had to have chemo and radiation treatments. My sister-in-law Nancy took me to many appointments and my sister Susan to the others. People at Roland Park Place appeared to enjoy the many hats that I wore, all of which were given to me by family and friends. When at last I began to grow hair, many people at Roland Park Place complimented me on my chemo curls, which are a big improvement over being bald.

Besides the moral support, I have found wonderful traveling companions at Roland Park Place. After Susan and I completed the work on the book, I went to Kenya and Tanzania with Nancy Bradford, a resident at Roland Park Place who was then eighty-five. We had a great time seeing the animals in the parks and visiting a Maasai village school. The courting rituals of lions especially intrigued us. Shortly after that trip, I made plans with another resident, Nancy Rouse, to go to seven national parks in the West, before I learned of my cancer diagnosis. Luckily, I finished radiation a little more than a week before we were scheduled to depart. Looking forward to the trip had been sustaining me while I went through treatments. Nancy and I had a great time, and I had no trouble keeping up with the group. In November 2014, I traveled again with Nancy Bedford, this time to Morocco, and we made plans to go to Guatemala and Costa Rica in 2015.

Obviously there are downsides to living in a continuing-care retirement community. Many people decline and die, and this can be depressing. I have to keep reminding myself that had I not moved into Roland Park Place, I never would have met the people who became the good friends I now miss. The staff works hard to help families cope with their relatives' decline, and those of us who knew the people are able to comfort the survivors. Just recently I heard from a new widow that her husband was able to be active until the end. I assured her that recalling Bert's ability to keep working and socializing until the end still comforts me, and I was sure it would do the same for her.

Once again, I have to say that I have no idea what the future will bring, but for now life at Roland Park Place seems very satisfactory. As Atul Gawande points out in *Being Mortal* (2014), retirement communities must do more than just keep old people safe. They also need to provide an atmosphere that can satisfy the emotional desires of very different people as they progress through their final years. Gerontologists have much to learn from the observations and insights of those of us who live in these communities.

REFERENCES

Gawande, Atul. 2014. *Being Mortal: Medicine and What Matters in the End*. New York: Metropolitan Books, Henry Holt and Company.

Annotated Bibliography of Further Reading

We offer the following additional readings related to residential options in later life, including retirement communities, nursing homes, continuing-care retirement communities, staying "in place" in one's own home, and living with adult offspring.

I. FICTION
(a chronological list compiled by Margaret Morganroth Gullette)

Who would have suspected there are already so many novels with late-life characters living, by choice or otherwise, in new domestic settings? Many writers use the living conditions of this age-based minority as a way of dramatically including material about desire, comradeship, and romance; serious social issues (power of attorney, elder fraud, assisted suicide, bureaucratic domination, ageist microaggressions, overmedication, the ageism of young children); philosophical themes (respect, autonomy, privacy, and personal/sexual freedom, personal authority, dignity); social class and poverty; and psychological issues (loneliness, boredom, mourning, conflicts with adult offspring over money, neglect, or the infliction of care). In many novels, disability becomes a nondefining attribute; "frailty" and cognitive impairment become less fearful.

Dying—known in administrative offices as "turnover"—seems not to provoke fear, but rarely occurs.

These novels are chronologically ordered because social and literary history influence writers. (The age at which they choose to write about old age may also be of interest.) More big-move novels have been published in recent decades, as the Age of Longevity bumps into Medicaid and the for-profit "care home," representing "untroublesome, steady investment in what's bound to be a growth industry," as a Joan Barfoot character observes. Overtly or subtly, many novels are protest literature. Yet there is little about caregivers' wages or state regulation of quality of care.

The books chosen here vary widely in style: some are highly praised literary fiction, others beach reading. Eccentricity or profundity abound, sometimes together between the same covers. Like World War II movies with one soldier of each ethnicity, the care community is a melting pot. More instances than one might expect are popular genre fiction—including the romance, featuring old people instead of young adults—another age-niche market. Although the subjectivity of older-adult protagonists agents would seem to be guaranteed (through dialogue, diaries, letters, or reported thoughts), this list excludes novels with a heavy ratio of backstory, because it implies that old adults have only memories rather than current interests, activities, and opinions. And some of these characters are just "real characters": cutesy cardboard.

Do the protagonists consider themselves "inmates," "residents," "tenants," or on the lam from the system? The "homes" tend to be one of two kinds. One, in which authorities survey, demean, and control the inmates, is the grim total institution. In the words of Ulla Kriebernegg, who is writing the first critical book about this literature, they are "detention centers for rebellious older characters to escape from" if they can. The other kind, where administrators are courteous and the food is good, is the conjoint living option with sociability, adventure, marriage, and psychological/moral development on offer. Many fantasies and actualities crisscross across the list.

There is no easy answer if your question is "What should *I* do?" except perhaps Robert Frost's "Provide, provide."

Austin, Jane. 1815. *Emma. London: John Murray.*

Not usually thought of as concerned with aging-in-place, this canonical novel of ethical development gives its young heroine not just singleness, nosiness, and a taste for matchmaking, but also a gentle valetudinarian father to care for—a parent easily bored, with fixed ideas, refusing anything unfamiliar, in a society where the word *senility* is never used and daughters and upright people carefully protect wealthy old men. Just as Emma is at her wit's end thinking she must live alone with her father for the rest of his life, their good and wealthy neighbor, Knightley, proves just how knightly he is by proposing and proposing to move himself into their house (not them into his): a fantasy romantic ending for 1815 or any era.

Lawrence, Josephine. 1934. *Years Are So Long. New York: Frederick A. Stokes Company.*

Written before Social Security was passed, when Lawrence's newspaper advice column often received questions such as "Do I have to support my parents?," this story of Ma and Pa Lear in Depression-era America finds Lucy and George Cooper (who lose their house when his factory closes) miserably divided in old age because their adult offspring refuse to take in both of them. The novel, which justifies a daughter-in-law's statement that "living to be old is the most dreadful fate in the world," was made into a 1937 movie *Make Way for Tomorrow*, directed by Leo McCarey. The bad old days that the two works highlighted helped make Social Security for a long time the third rail of American politics.

Updike, John. 1958. The Poorhouse Fair. New York: Fawcett Crest.

Updike set his carefully crafted debut novella, published when he was only twenty-six years old, on a single day in rural New Jersey's "Diamond County Home for the Aged" in order to focus on power relations and concepts of virtue in action among three characters: the coldly punctilious prefect, Conner; an irascible knee-jerk rebel, Gregg (age seventy); and a former teacher, Hook (ninety-four), who has survived his children and knows "how to be old." A true elder of illimitable calm, thoughtful speech, physical grace, and sensitivity to the pain of others, Hook's fine character and good health reflect Updike's admiration of his grandparents and his own interests in the atom bomb, President Buchanan, and ideas of heaven. Although nothing much happens at first—a cat is shot, the fair seems rained out—when the rain abates, a group of inmates gleefully flings small stones at Conner. He blames Hook, commits an act of petty tyranny against him, and is forgiven where the prefect had prided himself on forgiving. Since the 1950s, many writers far from old have also seen the rich possibilities in making an old-age "home" the setting for fiction.

Laurence, Margaret. (1964) 1993. The Stone Angel. Chicago: University of Chicago Press.

Hagar Shipley at ninety, with a tricky heart and a touchy pride, but a gift for first-person storytelling, has a current task: to stay in her own home after having mistakenly given it to her son and his wife, who, with the help of a doctor and a priest, are herding her toward an assisted-living placement from which people leave only "feet first." The suspense of the narrative depends on her attempts to escape this fate: when speech fails, by running away to live rough in an abandoned cannery. Interspersed with this tense material, Margaret Laurence gives Hagar a long autobiography of tribulation—set in the fictional Canadian countryside she calls Manawaka—about her childhood, rash marriage, childbirth and child-rearing, escape in midlife from her uncouth husband, and return to his Depression-era farm when he is dying. In this novel, which is more about character and late-life development than ageism, Hagar, turned to stone by grief, regret, and inability to express joy with anyone—has an epiphany in the hospital that enables her to accomplish the only two "truly free" things she has ever done.

Sarton, May. 1973. As We Are Now. New York: W. W. Norton.

This is the most angry, helpless, and vengeful of all the nursing-homes-are-prisons novels. Caroline (Caro) Spencer, a seventy-six-year-old retired schoolteacher, intelligent, sensitive, and physically frail, who has been moved by relatives into a ghastly rural Maine "home" and subjected to humiliations and un-relenting cruelty by the woman owner, even for doing good to fellow inmates and trying to hold onto a little joy for her-self. She winds up planning to burn down the institution and immolate herself, her captor, and everyone else in it. Without Caro Spencer's meditations and her adroit struggles against servile meekness, forgetfulness, and madness, written in the perplexed first person of a diary, the novel might be unbearable reading. Publication resulted in shutting down the nursing home that motivated the writing and, Sarton once said, inspired younger readers to visit older relatives in such places.

Carrington, Leonora. 1996. The Hearing Trumpet. Boston: Exact Change. Original French published 1974.

Carrington, a British surrealist, produced this strange classic of fantasy fiction when she was in her middle years. It is the first-person narrative of Marian Leatherby, a nearly deaf, bearded, and bewigged 92-year-old woman with a healthy mother of 110 and one impractical bosom friend. The novel begins at the point when the family locks Marian up in an unconventional, castle-like nursing home, "Santa Brigida," with a potential coven of witty, rebellious, and adventurous older women. A compendium of antiageist dialogues directed in part against the operators, Dr. and Mrs. Gambit, the novel segues into slapstick scenes of telepathy, a plot to outwit the Gambits' poisoned food, an earthquake, goddesses, and other *divertissements.*

Somers, Jane [pseud. for Doris Lessing]. 1983. The Diary of a Good Neighbor. In The Diaries of Jane Somers. New York: Vintage.

Janna, a well-to-do and rather selfish romance novelist, writes a first-person story about taking care of, then learning how to care for, and not being afraid of, a desperately poor woman who develops cancer. Maudie Fowler, who at first impression is "an old witch," "trembling with pride and dignity," lives in a sordid rent-controlled basement flat in London. Despite the travails of her disease, she wills herself to die at home. Along the way, she teaches Janna enough social history to enable her to upgrade her writing skills.

Wilder, Effie Leland (and, uncredited, Laurie Ellen Klein). 1995. Out to Pasture (But Not Over the Hill): A Short Novel. Carmel, NY: Guideposts.

Having lived nine years in a rural Presbyterian continuing-care community in South Carolina, eighty-five-year-old Wilder wrote this sweet-natured debut novel as a first-person diary-cum-letters by a seventy-eight-year-old woman full of her own opinions. She writes about a group of mainly idealized coresidents who seem to have few care needs, but who have "tiny adventures." They do good deeds for one another and the needy staff and keep it light about "becoming flaky," needing to cry, or dying. Wilder then wrote others in the series, including *Over What Hill? (Notes from the Pasture).*

Munro, Alice. 2002. "The Bear Came Over the Mountain," Hateship, Friendship, Courtship, Loveship, Marriage: Stories. New York: Vintage.

This is Nobel Prize–winner Munro's subtle short story (first published in 1999, when she was sxity-eight) about jealousy, definitions of marital fidelity, and memory loss. An Ontario nursing home is represented as a sociable place to meet new people and form new relationships. Fiona Andersson moves into a care facility, the comfortable, light-filled "Meadowlake," where she loses all memory of her formerly unfaithful husband, Grant. She becomes deeply attached to another man who is there only temporarily. Munro's focus is on Grant's behavior to make his wife's life satisfying in her new state, which involves doing what it takes to ensure she can see the new object of her affections. The story was made into a movie, *Away from Her* (2006), with Julie Christie as Fiona.

Weldon, Fay. 2002. *Rhode Island Blues*. New York: Grove Press.

In this clever bagatelle, the much-admired English feminist, Fay Weldon (age sixty-nine when she wrote the book), locates her rich, oft-widowed, tart-tongued eighty-ish protagonist, Felicity Moore, in settings where she or her grand-daughter Sophia can observe and rebut a rash of unashamedly greedy, controlling ageists, starting with the profit-sharing doctor and the jeering Nurse Dawn, who run Felicity's luxurious Rhode Island community, the "Golden Bowl Complex for Creative Retirement." By the end, both Sophia and Felicity have found true love. After wise pages about courtship and love in late adulthood, Felicity moves out of the broken Bowl to marry a seventy-two-year-old gambling addict she met at a funeral who enjoys sex as much as she does and is not after her Utrillo art work.

Edgerton, Clyde. 2004. *Lunch at the Piccadilly: A Novel*. New York: Ballantine Books.

This novel, by a prolific North Carolina comic writer, is almost farcical in its stereotyping of narrator Carl, a little man with a high voice who rarely dates, and his aunt Lil Olive, ensconced at the Rosehaven Convalescence Center and yearning to drive anywhere but Listre, North Carolina. Lil Olive provides not one but two scenes of preposterous driving behavior, one ending in a police pickup. Still, Carl is grateful to and genuinely cares for his only remaining relative and is fearful of the silence he will be left with when she dies. He spends a lot of time socializing with Lil and her friends. The many scenes of old women's verbal silliness and wit end in the composition of songs by two men. Some readers think the novel has "memorable characters"; others complain that it's just about "little old ladies and their zany adventures."

Barfoot, Joan. 2009. *Exit Lines*. London: Phoenix.

A novel about planning suicide in later life, the story is located in a relatively well-run upscale assisted-living facility, the "Idyll Inn," where former Children's Aid social worker Ruth Friedman, seventy-four, widowed and childless, suffering only from osteoporosis with no worse diagnosis, has found three mutually supportive friends. In the twenty-first–century Age of Longevity, "rational suicide" in fiction needs to be plausible, but Ruth's plan to die with her friends' help on her seventy-fifth birthday is undermotivated until a few pages from the end. Conversation and indirect speech allow us to follow the thinking of the other three about euthanasia, suffocation, and God, before each improbably agrees to assist. The prize-winning Canadian novelist Joan Barfoot (sixty-three when she published *Exit Lines*) wrote this before Canada passed an assisted dying law in 2014. The novel seems committed to resolutions, but its suspense about the value of living to Ruth suggests that despite Canada's cradle-to-grave health care system and the availability of hospice at the end of life, something in Western culture makes aging-into-the Fourth-Age seem more frightening than dying.

Casares, Oscar. 2009. Amigoland. Boston: Little, Brown and Company.

"Amigoland" is the unfriendly Brownsville, Texas, nursing home whose non-Spanish-speaking director refuses dinner to Don Fidencio, ninety-one, when he declines to wear a bib. Fidencios's seventy-year-old brother Celestino and his fortyish sweetheart, Socorro, soon arrive to spring him. They light out for the territory—their grandfather's property in Mexico. This is a fifty-five-year-old writer's debut novel about independent old men and succoring women that dares to stay mostly in the present, with Fidencio recounting the symptoms and bodily indignities that lead him on the short but difficult road trip to the truth that "he had escaped one prison only to discover that there was no way of escaping his own failing body." It ends just as Fidencio wishes, with distant family (a blind kinswoman and her grand-daughter) inviting him to stay for good.

Johnson, Todd. 2010. The Sweet By and By. New York: Harper.

This is another debut novel set (like Edgerton's *Lunch at the Piccadilly* and Jill McCorkle's *Life after Life*) in and around a North Carolina nursing home, with the narration dispersed among four characters talking in first-person Southern dialect. The two main characters are an African American nurse, Lorraine Bullock, who has affectionate relationships with the white residents ("I've seen every kind of old there is"), and a cranky purblind white resident, Margaret Clayton, in her nineties, who has increasing memory loss but thinks clearly, speaks humorously, describes her life in elegant speech, and increasingly depends on loyal Lorraine. The other two characters are Lorraine's daughter,

April, who becomes a doctor, and another young woman, Rhonda, who starts off afraid of the old people but finds Margaret an encouraging presence in her emotionally starved life. Multigenerational storytelling, with each woman given a race, a social class, and a turn at telling chapters, illuminates this community of women as "stately creatures ... perched around every bed where someone lies helpless."

McCorkle, Jill. 2013. *Life after Life. Chapel Hill, NC: Algonquin Books of Chapel Hill.*

Another novel set in North Carolina, *Life after Life* is remarkable for providing diverse, intersecting voices in and around a continuing-care retirement community: the notes of a hospice aide, the thoughts of the dying (or perhaps the recently deceased), the stories of a retired Jewish lawyer in her eighties who finds affection in an unexpected location (a man pretending to be "demented" and not doing a very good job of it), a fourteen-year-old who escapes from her dysfunctional family to visit a spiritual and peacemaking eighty four-year-old, and a twenty-something beautician who works in the community.

Sandlin, Tim. 2014. *Jimi Hendrix Turns Eighty. N.p.: Oothon Press.*

Sandlin (Oklahoma-born and fifty-seven when this was published) sets his satirical futuristic fantasy of collective rebellion and agency in a nursing home, "Mission Pescadero," in northern California in 2022. Hippie activists and one reflective misplaced Okie, Guy Fontaine, seethe about the tyrannical behavior of their own "Nurse Ratchet" and deploy their undiminished but disused skills to liberate the "high school hell all over again." They tar and feather the domineering director, expel the sedative-dispensing doctor, face down a cop boiling with Vietnam-era rage against hippies, and present the media, the sympathetic governor, and the world with a list of actual ageist evils.

II. MOSTLY NONFICTION
(an alphabetical list provided by Helen Q. Kivnick, Ruth Ray Karpen, and Anne M. Wyatt-Brown)

One cannot help but compare the messages about aging found in the fiction and nonfiction works we have selected. The potential problems that people face in late life include physical and mental disabilities, as well as ageist cultural attitudes that diminish the status of the older generation. The nonfiction scholarship about old-age living arrangements is sound, but the message is sometimes depressing. The novelists have an advantage in their ability to describe characters' youth and middle years, as well as their old age, so that we see the arc of an individual life and understand what has shaped a person over time. Some novelists create trilogies that interweave the life stories of many characters, told and retold from different perspectives, helping us see how one person's life affects and is affected by other people's lives over time.

Readers will find that there are many alternatives for living in later life, all of which provide challenges and opportunities. One message in this list is that feeling "at home," wherever one resides, is as much a psychological and emotional state as a physical one. One can feel at home most anywhere that feels safe and secure and where one finds comfort and peace. It is quite possible to create this environment in late life, but it requires preparation, a willingness to consider various options, and the ability to make changes while one is still relatively alert and active. The bottom line for us all is probably this: take courage and plan ahead for your old age.

Brody, Elaine. 2004. Women in the Middle: Their Parent Care Years. 2nd ed. New York: Springer.

Gerontologist Elaine Brody proved that President Ronald Reagan was wrong when he claimed that families no longer take care of the older generation. Her interviews of caregivers, however, demonstrate the financial and emotional burdens the caregivers face, even though they long to take care of their aging parents. Both the children and the parents experience a diminished social life. Partly as a result of her research, in widowhood Brody moved into a condo for older people rather than into the household of her children.

Butler, Katy. 2013. Knocking on Heaven's Door: The Path to a Better Way of Death. New York: Scribner.

In this memoir, a prize-winning journalist describes her parents' final years living and dying in their beloved Connecticut home. Everything changes for this healthy, vigorous couple when Jeffrey, a retired professor, suffers a crippling stroke at seventy-nine. He is sent home with a pacemaker, and Butler and her mother become his caregivers. Then her mother becomes gravely ill and refuses open-heart surgery, choosing to die the "old-fashioned" way, in her own time, without life-sustaining technologies. Butler issues a call for more vision, courage, and compassion in medical treatment, allowing patients to die more natural deaths at home on their own terms.

Cruikshank, Margaret. 2013. Learning to Be Old: Gender, Culture, and Aging. 3rd ed. Lanham, MD: Rowman and Littlefield Publishers, Inc.

Margaret Cruikshank, a feminist gerontologist, argues that in the United States, aging "is shaped more by culture than biology." If we are to age comfortably, we must learn to resist the social constructions that are harmful. Of course, she also recognizes that "our aging bodies matter greatly." We should, however, try to free ourselves from negative attitudes about physical decline and try to change social policy so that it works for "healthy aging." She thinks that cultural attitudes about older people cause families to place them in nursing homes where they are overmedicated. She argues that older people, especially women, should bond with other people of their age so that they can resist the denigration of the dominant culture. She devotes attention to class, ethnicity, sexual orientation, and gender, as well as ageism and countercultural gerontology. She thinks that the humanities can help older people see that they have a right to be in charge of their own future.

De Waal, Edmund. 2010. The Hare with Amber Eyes: A Hidden Inheritance. New York: Farrar, Straus and Giroux.

De Waal, born in 1964, is a well-known British ceramicist who spent a year in Japan listening to the family stories his eighty-four-year-old great-uncle told about their Austrian and French Jewish ancestors, some of whom had collected rare Japanese art (netsuke) and impressionist paintings. De Waal's effort to trace the origin of the artifacts turned into a journey of intergenerational discovery of a broken home and a family scattered by the Nazis. De Waal's story of displacement and loss is worth discussing in the context of this book.

Diamond, Timothy. 1992. Making Gray Gold: Narratives of
Nursing Home Care. Chicago: University of Chicago Press.

Sociologist Timothy Diamond began his research ten years
before this book was published. For six months, he trained
to become a certified nursing aide. Then he worked in three
different nursing homes in Chicago for periods of three to
four months each. For years after, he analyzed his field notes,
read relevant literature, visited other homes across the United
States to validate and update his findings, and wrote this book.
The result is a compelling inside story of what it was like to
work and live in a nursing home in the 1980s. In Diamond's
words, it is "a collective story told by the residents and the
nursing assistants I came to know." It is also a critique of the
commodification of nursing care, where corporate entities get
rich while the people who actually provide the care struggle
to live on a minimum wage. This is one of the first research-
based arguments for nursing-home reform, based on both
ethnographic research and a critical analysis of health care
documents.

Gardam, Jane. 2004. Old Filth. London: Chatto and
Windus.

In this first book of a trilogy, the protagonist, Edward Feathers, known as Filth (Failed in London Try Hong-Kong), becomes a successful international lawyer despite his miserable
childhood. As a child, he was deracinated: his mother died
following his birth, and he lived with his father in Malaya, but
his father paid no attention to him. At four-and-a-half, he was
sent to a Welsh home for "Raj orphans"—children of British
civil servants who were sent back to England and preschool
foster care. The woman who ran the home abused him. At

eight, he went to prep school and later to university. Despite living in Hong Kong for most of his adult years, he never felt at home there. He returns to England in retirement, but he does not feel very English either. Near the end of his life, he learns that he was not responsible for the death of the abusive Welsh woman despite having thought so for most of his life. Freed from unearned guilt, he journeys exuberantly to his birthplace, the only place he has ever thought of as home, where he unexpectedly dies.

Gardam, Jane. 2009. The Man in the Wooden Hat.
New York: Europa Editions.

The second novel in the trilogy tells the story of Edward Feather's marriage from his wife's perspective. Betty, who was born in China, has also lived all over the world. During World War II, she lived in a Japanese internment camp, where her parents died. After the war, she moves to Hong Kong, where she meets Eddie Feather and accepts his proposal. That same evening, she meets Terry Veneering, whom Feather despises, and immediately the two feel an attraction. She has one intense night with Veneering, which leads to a pregnancy and eventual miscarriage. Albert Ross, Feather's solicitor (the man in the wooden hat), discovers her infidelity and confronts her. The person Betty loves best turns out to be Harry, Veneering's young son. After her marriage, she lives with Feather in Hong Kong and then returns with him to England, where they see other expatriates who have also lived in the Far East so long that they no longer feel at home in England. Natives of Hong Kong, however, have mostly ignored the British. Betty stays with Edward but contemplates leaving him after Harry dies. Instead of leaving, she dies unexpectedly.

Gardam, Jane. 2013. Last Friends. New York: Europa Editions.

The third book in the trilogy, *Last Friends*, depicts the childhood and later life of Veneering, Betty's one-time lover and Feather's late-life neighbor. Veneering's early life was also a story of displacement. Neither of his parents was accepted by middle-class English society. Veneering was identified early as being very intelligent, which meant that he had an education despite losing his parents during the war. Still, he couldn't get a job once he finished his legal training. Like Feathers, he practiced in the Far East. Betty Feathers was the love of his life, along with his son, Harry. Once Veneering and Feather die, their old friends, Fiscal-Smith and Dulcie, are left behind. Both are lonely; like all the people they have known, they do not feel at home in Hong Kong or in England. At the novel's end, there is hope that they might find solace in each other's company. The characters' stories in this trilogy are closely interwoven because they constitute a tightly knit group of English people who lived most of their lives in Hong Kong. Among other themes, the novels explore the meaning of national identity and its connection to individual identity and one's sense of place and purpose in the world.

Gass, Thomas Edward. 2004. Nobody's Home: Candid Reflections of a Nursing Home Aide. Ithaca, NY: Cornell University Press.

In this memoir, Gass draws on his own experiences, first as a nursing aide and then as director of social services at a privately owned, for-profit long-term care facility in the Midwest. He concludes that we need to change the ways we think about, run, staff, and finance nursing homes because "our current system does not normally bring out the best in those involved." Less analytical than the scholarly ethnographers, Gass describes daily life in the nursing home in the vernacular of those who live and work there.

Gawande, Atul. 2014. Being Mortal: Medicine and What Matters in the End. London: Profile Books.

Atul Gawande uses real-life stories to present his medical perspective on death and dying. His personal experience with his father's final days, as well as his own visits and interviews with other older people, have helped shape his attitude toward the physician's role in working with elders. Although his medical training had encouraged him to extend life regardless of the consequences, he came to understand that patients have the right to make their own decisions. He found it important to grant patients' autonomy to live where and how they choose, rather than overemphasizing the importance of safety and longevity.

Golant, Stephen M. 2015. Aging in the Right Place. Baltimore: Health Professions Press.

Stephen Golant says that today's elders encounter a "persistent stay-at-home message" everywhere they turn. In contrast, he explores the many possible housing arrangements available. He encourages older people to consider other alternatives when they are dissatisfied with their current living arrangements. He devotes chapters to aging in place with paid help, clustered housing solutions, senior cohousing developments, independent living, assisted living developments, and continuing-care retirement communities. He describes the advantages and disadvantages of each alternative and interviews individuals to find out their emotional reactions to these housing choices.

**Gubrium, Jaber. 1975. *Living and Dying at Murray Manor.*
New York: St. Martin's.**

For this classic ethnographic study, sociologist Jay Gubrium spent several months observing and participating in a nursing home called Murray Manor. He focuses on how people in their various roles—residents (whom he calls "clientele"), staff, physicians, administrators, and family—negotiate their needs and goals, creating a unique social environment. Gubrium gives readers a feel for what it's like to work and live in a nursing home, particularly in terms of performing daily "bed and body work," passing the time, and facing death and dying. Gubrium nicely illustrates how an undifferentiated place like a nursing home gains meaning through the daily routines of the people who live and work there.

**Halgrim Seaver, Anna Mae. 1994. "*My World Now: Life in
a Nursing Home, from the Inside.*" Newsweek, June 27, 11.
(Reprinted widely online.)**

In this short article, found by the author's son and published in *Newsweek* after her death, the eighty-four-year-old author reflects on her life in a nursing home. In an honest and engaging voice, the former teacher describes herself and other residents, their physical changes, the loss of privacy, and the indignities of being infantilized by diapers and baby-talking staff. Simply and poignantly, she chronicles a typical day and compares it to days gone by: "What is today, again? The afternoon drags into early evening. This used to be my favorite time of the day. Things would wind down. I would kick off my shoes. Put my feet up on the coffee table and enjoy the fruits of my day's labor with my husband. He's gone. So is my health. *This* is my world."

Hazan, Haim. 1992. *Managing Change in Old Age: The Control of Meaning in an Institutional Setting*. Albany: State University of New York Press.

Written by a professor of sociology and social anthropology at Tel Aviv University, this ethnographic study examines everyday life in an old age home in Israel. Hazan explores the interconnection of the nursing home, the network of agencies dealing with old age, and the complex culture and politics of Israel. At the time of the study, there were three categories of publicly run old-age homes in Israel. The home represented in the study serves only able-bodied residents who have transitioned from community-based life to an institutional setting. "Managing change" for this group includes manipulating the physical boundaries and bureaucratic practices of the institution and developing and maintaining relationships, personal identity, and existential meaning. Hazan describes the paradoxes of life in a nursing home, the result of which, for many residents, is a "disorganized, amorphous view of the world."

Horner, Joyce. 1982. *That Time of Year: A Chronicle of Life in a Nursing Home*. Boston: University of Massachusetts Press.

Joyce Horner taught English at Mount Holyoke College in Massachusetts, where she retired as a full professor in 1969. Having published two novels and several poems in leading magazines, she had an abiding love of "good literature" and "the structure of the English sentence in fine prose and poetry." But after she broke several bones in a fall, combined with arthritis, she became a semi-invalid in need of care. She entered a nursing home, and from 1975 to 1977 chronicled her thoughts, feelings, and experiences. She shows her sensitivity to "the details and varieties of human life and art," while striving to be "accurate and honest" about the ups and downs of life in a nursing home.

Kane, Robert L., and Joan C. West. 2005. It Shouldn't Be This Way: The Failure of Long-Term Care. Nashville: Vanderbilt University Press.

Robert Kane, a physician with expertise in long-term care and aging, and his sister Joan West, an educator and the principal caregiver for their mother during the time described in the book, chronicle their own struggles to find quality care for their mother after she suffered a stroke. She spent the last years of her life in care facilities, first a rehabilitation facility, then an assisted-living facility, and finally a nursing home. The authors describe their mother's experiences in these places and end each chapter with a list of lessons they learned about the long-term care system. They also include a chapter on "informal care"—that provided at home by unpaid family and friends—which they point out does not end once the frail elder moves to a facility. Kane and West offer much practical advice in this highly informative book that will help readers better understand and respond to the issues they will face in selecting a care facility for themselves or a loved one.

Kidder, Tracy. 1991. Old Friends. Boston: Houghton Mifflin.

In this true story, which reads like a novel, Pulitzer Prize–winning author Tracy Kidder shows us daily life in a nursing home through the eyes of roommates Lou and Joe. Though strangers when thrust together in a room at Linda Manor, the two become close friends while struggling with the past, their present circumstances, and the future. From the book jacket: "*Old Friends* is laced with comedy, sometimes with gentle wit, sometimes with farce. In the end, it reminds us of the great continuities, of the possibilities for renewal in the face of mortality, of the survival to the very end of all that is truly essential about life."

McMillan, Terry. 1995. "Ma'Dear." In Children of the Night: The Best Short Stories by Black Writers 1967–the Present, edited by Gloria Naylor, 423–33. New York: Little, Brown and Company.

This short story was the precursor to McMillan's book *Mama*. It is a first-person narrative told in the voice of a feisty, funny seventy-two-year-old African American widow trying to make ends meet on her Social Security check. She takes in student boarders so she can keep her "big old house," but they are rarely home, and she is often lonely. Her friends live in nursing homes and can't visit, so she goes to the park, the beauty shop, or the movies, where she eavesdrops and observes others. The one person she talks to on a regular basis is the person who worries her the most—her caseworker, whom she suspects of looking for ways to reduce her pension.

Neuman, Maryla, as told to Fred Amram. 2012. Pockets in My Soul. United States of America: Maryla Neuman.

Raised as an advantaged Jewish child in Lwów, Poland, in the 1920s and 1930s, Maryla Neuman survived the Soviet and Nazi invasions, displacement to the Lwów ghetto, hiding on a farm, two prisons, and two concentration camps. After four years in a displaced persons camp, she, together with her husband and young son, were sponsored to resettle in the United States. Neuman was nearly ninety when she wrote this memoir. Unlike the stories told by younger genocide survivors, hers comes to us through the lens of a long lifetime of experience. Yes, it is a personal account of the Holocaust, and of a new, free life in the United States. Yes, her life has included skeins of privilege, terror, loss, love, luck, sorrow, and success—all woven on a warp of determination and ingenuity. But still, in her own very old age, she lives with the despairs that did not end with Liberation and the beginning of a new life in America. She works to articulate lessons learned from early life experience with genocide, at the same time as she struggles to create later-life wisdom from an adulthood of vicissitudes not atypical of twentieth-century, urban American women.

Pym, Barbara. 1977. *Quartet in Autumn. New York: Penguin Books.*

In this Booker Prize–nominated novel, Barbara Pym introduces four aging London office workers   two women and two men. The four chat in the same office but are not friends outside it. Each of the four lives alone. One man and one woman occupy houses that had, earlier in their lives, been their family homes. Of the four, only the woman who rents a small, one-room apartment has made specific retirement plans—to move to the country and share the home of a long-time, single friend. These plans are disrupted by two unexpected events: the sale of her apartment building to a new owner-occupant whose large family she knows she will not be able to abide, and her country friend's unexpected engagement to a new, younger man in her town. Both women retire some years before the men, confronting all four with issues of uncertain social supports and personal intimacies, increasing physical fragility, and the need to restructure daily life and meaning systems in response to the disruption of their longstanding routines and expectations. The individual stories are quiet and undramatic—as the lives of so many elders must appear to those who know only their outer appearances. What is friendship? Responsibility? Contribution? Caring? And what do these mean to individuals who grow old without close ties to friends, family, occupation, or community?

Ray, Ruth. 2008. Endnotes: An Intimate Look at the End of Life. New York: Columbia University Press.

This is the true story of a forty-two-year-old gerontologist, Ruth Ray (Karpen), who facilitates a writing group in a nursing home and develops a relationship with Paul, an eighty-two-year-old member of the group. The book chronicles their growing relationship against the backdrop of nursing home life. A surprising and compelling love story, *Endnotes* also provides a thoughtful reflection on aging and ageism, sex and gender dynamics in the nursing home, death and dying, the ethics of caregiving, and the nature of knowledge making in gerontology. In a chapter titled "Home," Ray describes, from the perspective of Paul, what makes a place feel like home and the social and emotional challenges of making a nursing home one's final residence.

Ray, Ruth, and Toni Calasanti, eds. 2011. Nobody's Burden: Lessons from the Great Depression on the Struggle for Old-Age Security. Lanham, MD: Lexington.

Drawing on an archive of case files kept by geriatric social workers from 1925 to 1934, the authors describe what it was like to grow old at home, in the homes of family members, or in boarding houses and rented rooms in Detroit during the Great Depression. The book describes the meager public and private assistance available to older adults before the advent of unemployment insurance, Social Security, Medicare, and Medicaid. Looming over clients was the specter of the local poor house, which in 1933 housed fourteen thousand residents, many of them over the age of sixty. Case studies of selected clients illustrate the struggles and triumphs of older men and women trying to sustain a home and a sense of personal freedom and financial security without becoming a burden to others.

Robinson, Marilynne. 2004. Gilead. New York: Farrar, Straus, Giroux.

The three novels of Marilynne Robinson tell two intertwined family stories. The first is narrated by the Reverend John Ames, a Congregationalist minister, seventy-six, whose wife Lila is forty-one and his son Robby is six. Rev. Ames has been told that he will die soon, so in 1957, he begins to write about his life as a testament to his young son. Most of his thoughts consist of remembering the adventures of his grandfather and father, who were also ministers. At the end of his life, Ames feels personally grounded in Gilead, Iowa, and in his profession as a Congregational minister.

Robinson, Marilynne. 2008. Home. New York: Farrar, Straus, Giroux.

Home, the second novel in the trilogy, features the Reverend Robert Boughton, Ames's best friend, who has lost his wife and is estranged from his favorite son. Like Ames, Boughton is very ill and needs hands-on care. Although Boughton's five other children visit and take turns caring for him, his heart yearns for Jack, the prodigal son, who temporarily returns in 1956 after an absence of twenty years. Boughton and his children think of Gilead, Iowa, as home, but they are all aware that being in the family house does not compensate for their sense of loss. After a few weeks, Jack leaves once again, just before his African American wife and child drive up in a car looking for him. At the end, Glory, the daughter, is left behind to care for her ailing father and to long for another visit from Jack.

Robinson, Marilynne. 2014. *Lila*. New York: Farrar, Straus, Giroux.

Lila tells the story of John Ames's young wife, whose hardscrabble upbringing bears no resemblance to those of the rest of Ames's genteel parishioners. Lila has no home. As a baby she was stolen by Doll, a drifter who keeps her alive. The two roam around the countryside hunting for work. Unexpectedly one day, Lila walks into a church in Gilead, Iowa, and for the first time finds a sense of peace. She continues to live rough but attends church and eventually marries the much older John Ames. Throughout the novel both John and Lila know that she and her son Robby will not live in Gilead forever. Lila expects to leave once John dies. The characters are aware of their own aging and that of their friends and family members, but the author's emphasis is on the humanity of her protagonists. The young wife realizes that her husband is old, but she keeps saying that he is beautiful. Neither aging nor dying is an entirely negative experience as Robinson interprets them.

Ross, Jennie-Keith. 1977. *Old People New Lives: Community Creation in a Retirement Residence*. Chicago: University of Chicago Press.

American anthropologist Jennie-Keith Ross lived for one year as a participant-observer in a French retirement home, Les Floralies, which had just been built for Parisian construction workers and their wives or widows. Ross shows how the residents, initially strangers to one another, created a complex community with a social structure and status system, community norms, conflicting factions, and a socialization process for new residents. Ross concludes that the retirement community offers many social and emotional benefits to elder residents, including various avenues for expressing independence, developing status among peers, participating socially, building friendships and intimate relationships, and assisting others in times of need.

Sacks, Oliver. 2015. *On the Move: A Life*. New York: Alfred A. Knopf.

In this autobiography of resilience, neurologist and author Oliver Sacks, who died at eighty-two shortly after the book was printed, is remarkably candid about his life, his loves, the various places he has lived and worked, and the people he has known. We learn of his guilt over leaving his family in Great Britain to come to America. He writes of his past use of illegal drugs and his moments of emotional turmoil. He describes the origin of his many books on illness and disability. In a later article, Sacks talks of the joy he felt, correcting the galleys of this memoir while recovering from a painful procedure connected with unexpected terminal cancer. When the pain subsided, once again he began to anticipate "impending adventures."

The overall impression Sacks leaves us with is that being at home or "in place" in the world depends, for him, on the ability to explore his interests and express his creativity.

Thomas, William H. 1996. Life Worth Living: How Someone You Love Can Still Enjoy Life in a Nursing Home. Acton, MA: VanderWyk and Burnham.

In this initial exploration of what he calls the "Eden Alternative," geriatric physician William Thomas proposes a new way of designing nursing homes to ensure that they are "human habitats" where residents, regardless of their health status, can still enjoy life. In response to what he has observed as the three common "plagues" of nursing homes—loneliness, helplessness, and boredom—Thomas advocates for institutional environments that empower staff and residents to participate equally in caring for themselves and other people, as well as plants and animals.

Thomas, William. 2004. What Are Old People For? Acton, MA: VanderWyk and Byrnham.

Thomas has now moved beyond the Eden Alternative to advocate for abolishing nursing homes entirely. He considers the nursing home, a corporate-run business that slickly markets its products to specific clientele, "the bizarre ultimate end point of the consumer lifestyle." Instead, Thomas proposes "Green Houses"—intentional communities consisting of various types of homes where older people of all ability levels live and learn together, assist one another, and provide an example of shared responsibility to younger generations. Thomas envisions these communities as small "sanctuaries for elderhood" that are cooperative, nonhierarchically structured, and founded on shared beliefs, among them using technology in a "smart" way, staying connected with the natural world, and continuing to develop through the end of life.

Wallis, Velma. 1993. Two Old Women: An Alaska Legend of Betrayal, Courage and Survival. 10th anniversary ed. New York: HarperCollins.

In this inspiring novella, Wallis retells an Athabascan Indian legend, begun "long before the arrival of Western culture," and passed along for generations from mothers to daughters. It is the story of two old women, weak and dependent, abandoned by their tribe during a winter famine. Rather than give into death, the women decide to "die trying" to survive the harsh environment. They rely on each other's strengths and begin to recall old skills as they build shelter, trap animals, and struggle to provide for themselves. Overcoming enormous odds, the women not only survive but flourish. The following year, now strong in body, mind, and spirit, they help their returning tribe by teaching what they have learned about survival. In Wallis's words, the story shows "that there is no limit to one's ability—certainly not age—to accomplish in life what one must."

ANNE M. WYATT-BROWN is Associate Professor Emeritus in the Program in Linguistics, University of Florida. She was the editor of Age Studies, a book series for the University Press of Virginia, and coeditor of the *Journal of Aging, Humanities, and the Arts*, sponsored by the Gerontological Society of America. She is the author of *Barbara Pym: A Critical Biography* and a coedited collection (with Janice Rossen), *Aging and Gender in Literature: Studies in Creativity*. Her essays and articles have appeared in *The Gerontologist; Generations; Journal of Aging Studies; Aging and Identity; Psychohistory Review; The Journal of Modern Literature; Handbook of the Humanities and Aging; Encyclopedia of Gerontology: Age, Aging, and the Aged*, second edition; and *A Guide to Humanistic Studies in Aging*.

MARGARET MORGANROTH GULLETTE is an internationally known age critic, nonfiction writer, and essayist. Her latest books are *Agewise: Fighting the New Ageism in America*, a 2012 winner of the Eric Hoffer Book Award, and *Aged by Culture*, a Noteworthy Book of the Year (*Christian Science Monitor*). Her book on the midlife, *Declining to Decline*, received the Emily Toth Award as the best feminist book on American popular culture. Gullette's essays are often cited as notable in *Best American Essays*, and she is a winner of the Daniel Singer Millennial Prize. She writes frequently for the mainstream and feminist press. She is a Resident Scholar at the Women's Studies Research Center, Brandeis University.

RUTH RAY KARPEN is Professor Emeritus in the College of Liberal Arts at Wayne State University in Detroit. She is author of *Beyond Nostalgia: Aging and Life Story Writing* and *Endnotes: An Intimate Look at the End of Life*, along with many chapters and articles on women's aging, late-life writing, and feminist gerontology. She is coeditor, with Thomas R. Cole and Robert Kastenbaum, of the *Handbook of the Humanities and Aging*, second edition, and *A Guide to Humanistic Studies in Aging*. She is also coeditor, with Toni Calasanti, of *Nobody's Burden: Lessons from the Great Depression on the Struggle for Old-Age Security*.

HELEN Q. KIVNICK, PHD, LP, is Professor of Social Work at the University of Minnesota. She is the Humanities and Arts editor for *The Gerontologist* and a former Master Teaching Artist for the National Center for Creative Aging. Dr. Kivnick is best known for writing, programming, and teaching that integrate aging, lifespan development, music and the arts, and social justice. In particular, she is recognized for her collaboration with renowned scholar Erik H. Erikson on the book *Vital Involvement in Old Age*. Trained as a clinical psychologist, Kivnick has worked for over thirty years to promote healthy life-cycle development, vital involvement, and the arts and intercultural relations.